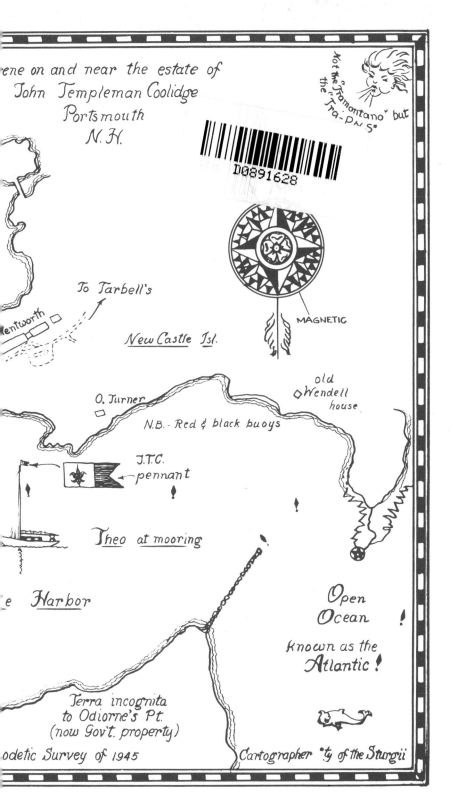

...ene on and near the estate of
John Templeman Coolidge
Portsmouth
N. H.

Not the "Tramontano" but the "Tra-P-N-S"

MAGNETIC

To Tarbell's

Wentworth

New Castle Isl.

O. Turner

old Wendell house.

N.B. - Red & black buoys

J.T.C. pennant

Theo at mooring

...e Harbor

Open Ocean !

known as the Atlantic !

Terra incognita
to Odiorne's Pt.
(now Gov't. property)

...odetic Survey of 1945

Cartographer 'ty of the Sturgii

Once I Was Very Young

MOLLY COOLIDGE IN THE MANSION'S COUNCIL CHAMBER
Courtesy of Betsy Baybutt

Once I Was Very Young

by

MARY COOLIDGE PERKINS

with a New Introduction
by
Woodard D. Openo, Ph.D.

Published for the
Wentworth-Coolidge Commission

by
PETER E. RANDALL PUBLISHER
PORTSMOUTH, NEW HAMPSHIRE
2000

Endleaves: Map drawn by cartographer Dorothy Harding Sturgis
(1891-1978), daughter of the architect R. Clipston Sturgis. Dorothy
lived for many years at the Martine Cottage at Little Harbor.

Additional copies available from
Wentworth-Coolidge Commission
375 Little Harbor Road
Portsmouth, NH 03801

Peter E. Randall Publisher
Box 4726, Portsmouth, NH 03802

Library of Congress Cataloging-in-Publication Data
Perkins, Mary Coolidge
    Once I was very young / by Mary Coolidge Perkins ; with a new intro-
duction by Woodard D. Openo.
    p.cm.
ISBN 0-914339-88-5 (alk. paper)
1. Perkins, Mary Coolidge--Childhood and youth.
2. Portsmouth (N.H.)--Biography. I. Title.
CT275.P5717 A3 2000
974.2'6--dc21
[B]
                                                              99-056335

ACKNOWLEDGMENTS

In the 100 years since Molly Coolidge Perkins was a child spending summers at Little Harbor, the property she loved, today known as the Wentworth-Coolidge Mansion, has seen many transformations. Raised in a household that valued art, culture, history, and storytelling, Molly and her siblings learned to treasure a sense of the past that was embraced by all the friends and family who spent time at Little Harbor during the Colonial Revival era. Molly was 73 in 1954 when her step-mother, Mary Abigail Parsons Coolidge, decided to donate the Mansion and the property to the state of New Hampshire in honor of the late J. Templeman Coolidge.

At age 79, Molly published this memoir of her childhood at Little Harbor for her grandchildren. These stories capture the essence of that time and it seems especially appropriate to reprint them now, as the Wentworth-Coolidge Commission is increasing its efforts to make the site accessible to the public and to keep these stories alive, as well as stories about Royal Governor Benning Wentworth. Currently, the Commission sponsors tours, lectures, concerts, exhibits, student internships, a New Hampshire History program for elementary students, and an annual Lilac Festival. To connect with the artistic tradition established at the site by the Coolidge family, the Commission now sponsors year-round art classes and contemporary art exhibits in the Coolidge Visitors' Center. The Wentworth-Coolidge Mansion is on its way to becoming more central—once again—to the cultural, historical, and artistic life of the Piscataqua Region.

While several members of the Coolidge family have been generous and helpful throughout the process of getting this book

WENTWORTH-COOLIDGE MANSION IN THE 1930S
Courtesy of Betsy Baybutt

reprinted, special thanks go to Betsy Baybutt, grand-daughter of
J. Templeman and niece of Molly, who has been a constant source
of inspiration and encouragement. Like Molly Coolidge, Betsy also
spent many summers during her childhood at Little Harbor. She
has kept many of her memories alive by sharing them with us. Betsy
also loaned to the Wentworth-Coolidge Commission many of
her family photographs. Several of these (some of which appear
in this new edition) were taken by Molly beginning at age 14.

Catherine A. Vaillancourt, a graduate student in History at
the University of New Hampshire, has spent the past year research-
ing the Coolidge family. She also designed the exhibit entitled
"Artistic Retreat: The Coolidge Family at Little Harbor, 1886-1954"
at the Portsmouth Athenaeum in January, 2000 before being
installed at the Coolidge Visitors' Center. Molly Coolidge Perkins'
relatives, Mrs. Malcolm D. Perkins, Mr. & Mrs. Samuel Perkins,
Mrs. Judith Coolidge Jones, and Mrs. Henry Parsons Coolidge welcomed Catherine into their homes to look at old photographs
and to hear their stories. Catherine brought this whole project
together and has made a tangible contribution to the interpre-

tation of the Coolidge's enduring impact on this site. This project involved the work of many individuals, but it was Catherine who made it happen.

All of this effort would have gone unnoticed without the generous financial support of Charlotte Lyman Fardelmann and Betsy Baybutt. Charlotte, who for the past thirty-eight years has lived in the converted "Hennery" next door to the Mansion, is an artist and author, and has always appreciated the historical significance of this site. Betsy Baybutt, an artist of many talents, has helped us all remember what this Mansion and piece of shoreline meant to her family. The Wentworth-Coolidge Commission is especially grateful to both Charlotte and Betsy, whose offer to underwrite the re-printing expenses of *Once I Was Very Young* has guaranteed that Molly Coolidge's childhood stories will remain a vital connection between the past and the future at the Wentworth-Coolidge Mansion.

Molly Bolster
Director
Wentworth-Coolidge Mansion

JACK, KATRINE, AND ELIZABETH COOLIDGE AT LITTLE HARBOR.
Photograph by Molly Coolidge
Courtesy of Betsy Baybutt

INTRODUCTION

Mary ("Molly") Coolidge married John Forbes Perkins of Milton, Massachusetts, on September 6, 1905, in the Wentworth Mansion at Little Harbor. Their children were Katherine (b.1907), John Forbes (b.1909) and Malcolm Donald (b.1914). Katherine died in 1920, so the grandchildren to whom the book is dedicated are the children of the two sons. As a young adult, Molly studied clay modeling with the sculptor Bela Pratt at the Museum School in Boston and design with Joseph Lindon Smith, who is mentioned in the book. She died in 1962 and her husband in 1964.

One can see how Molly's background could stimulate a creative spirit. Her father, John Templeman Coolidge III ("Templeman"), graduated from Harvard College in 1879 and married Katherine Scollay Parkman, daughter of the great Boston historian, Francis Parkman. As their descendants delight in remarking, "They went to Paris on their honeymoon, spent six years there and returned with two daughters." While in Paris, Templeman studied art in the studio of Carolus Duran where he met the rising American artist, John Singer Sargent, who would become a lifelong friend. A fellow student in Paris was Arthur Astor Carey, whom Templeman had known at Harvard.

In addition to Arthur Carey, other close Harvard friends included Barrett Wendell, Alexander Wadsworth Longfellow, Jr., (nephew of the poet Henry Wadsworth Longfellow and a fellow member of the Art Club at Harvard), and the brothers Edmund and John Wheelwright. All of them were interested in history, two (Edmund Wheelwright and "Waddy" Longfellow) became architects, and at least one (Longfellow) was, like Coolidge, an avid sailor.

J. TEMPLEMAN COOLIDGE PAINTING HIS DAUGHTER
Collection of the State of New Hampshire and the Wentworth-Coolidge Commission

When the Coolidges returned from Europe in 1885, they were attracted to the Wentworth Mansion that was for sale by its eccentric owner, William P. Israel. Although well-known by the public for its romantic colonial history, and sketched by Boston architects, the Mansion had been used as a farmhouse for most of the nineteenth century and was, according to Henry Coolidge, quite dilapidated when his father bought it the following year. However, it proved to be a paradise for children and a source of endless fascination for its new owner, who frequently guided visitors—even strangers who showed up at the door—through it. In 1887, Arthur Carey bought the adjacent property, which he called "Creek Farm"; it included the mid-eighteenth century

Martine Cottage (a "Cape" or 1&1/2 story cottage in the regional vernacular), which he sold to the Boston architect, R. Clipston Sturgis, in 1890. Both Creek Farm and the Martine Cottage can be seen from Wentworth Road, across Sagamore Creek.

Another Harvard friend with a young family was Barrett Wendell, hired as an English instructor at the College in 1880. Although he had grown up in New York City, the Wendell family was from Portsmouth and relatives still occupied the homestead there. In 1882, Barrett's father, Jacob, built a house in New Castle designed by Edmund Wheelwright, who designed a house for Edmund Clarence Stedman on nearby Wild Rose Lane shortly thereafter. Templeman, urged on by his Uncle John Coolidge, had to extend himself to buy the Mansion, neglected though it was, and few of his friends would have considered themselves rich. By contrast, Arthur Astor Carey was the great-grandson of the fabulously wealthy John Jacob Astor; as such, he had money and European social connections which tended to set him apart from his Little Harbor neighbors.

As noted, Templeman Coolidge was most interested in art and architecture, history, and boats. He greatly admired the paintings of Edmund C. Tarbell and Frank Benson. They began visiting the Portsmouth area around 1889 and are believed to have rented a house on Wild Rose Lane in New Castle, facing Little Harbor near the Wentworth Hotel. In 1905, Tarbell bought an old house near the causeway to Portsmouth and made it his home. Finally, it should be noted that a surprising number of the Little Harbor summer colonists had lived in France. This was a considerable advantage in their day, French being the international language as English is now.

A few comments on references in the stories may help to clarify them. In "The Box," Molly talks about the Mulloons living on Leaches Island, the large island opposite the Mansion. She later built a cottage there. The island is now owned by the State of New Hampshire and is uninhabited; no structures remain, although some foundations can be found. "The Tiny Sailboat"

PETER THE PRINCE. Photograph by Molly Coolidge
Courtesy of Betsy Baybutt

WOOD SPRITES—ELIZABETH AND JACK COOLIDGE.
Photograph by Molly Coolidge
Courtesy of Betsy Baybutt

was built by Crosby; and Crosby "cats" (boats with a single sail) are still well-known in New England. In "The Circus," the Wendell children were Barrett Wendell, Jr., born on April 19, 1881, and his sister Mary Barrett Wendell, born on February 17, 1883. Their parents were Barrett and Edith Greenough Wendell. In "Horse," Patsy Shea's father is mentioned as having a farm; apparently he was the tenant in the Martine Cottage and a photo of ca.1890 shows him standing in front of it. The "Crazy Woman" was reported on Little Harbor Road while Molly was at Grandma Cushing's house; Grandma Cushing lived in the house to the right as one approaches the water on that road and was not really a relative of the Coolidges. In "School," "Mrs. Gardner" is Isabella Stewart Gardner, who was married to Templeman's Uncle John Gardner; she was a legendary art collector who built a mansion in the form of a Venetian palace on The Fenway in Boston to house her collection. After her death, it became the Gardner Museum, which it remains today.

"The Gift Tree" alludes to Molly's considerable talents as a photographer (a partial collection of her photographs is housed at the Library at Strawbery Banke Museum in Portsmouth). "Grampa and Indian Play" portrays the elderly Francis Parkman, the historian of the French and English conflict in North America, finishing his life's work at the Mansion and taking time out to teach Molly a hard lesson about fishing. "Cruising on Theo" relates the Coolidges' love of the sea and suggests Molly's competence as a sailor; the reader should note that the "boys" enumerated at Marblehead Race Week could not have included Henry Wadsworth Longfellow; "Alexander Wadsworth Longfellow, Jr.," must have been meant. "Japanese Play at Dublin" features Joseph Lindon Smith, artist, archaeologist and, with his wife Corinna, enthusiastic producer of very accomplished amateur plays; they had a summer home at Dublin, New Hampshire. The summer colony there was considerably more social than that at Little Harbor, and it has been said that Katherine Parkman Coolidge preferred its activity to the Portsmouth colony, where one had to make

JACK AND ELIZABETH AT TEA. Photograph by Molly Coolidge
Courtesy of Betsy Baybutt

one's own amusement. Finally, "Countess Obendorff and Others" tells of Molly's encounters with Arthur Astor Carey's relatives; clearly, to Molly, growing up in Little Harbor and Boston was the best of all possible worlds and she wouldn't have traded it for anything. That is the message that comes through in these stories, which make good reading for children and adults. Along the way, they provide a glimpse into the life of a very talented child who had the best sort of education a century ago, being blessed with understanding and slightly unconventional parents.

The children of Katherine Parkman and John Templeman Coolidge were Mary ("Molly") born in Paris, France, on May 23, 1881; Katherine Parkman ("Katrine") Coolidge, born in Paris on January 5, 1883; Louise Riche, born on August 19, 1886; John Templeman Coolidge, Jr., born on December 28, 1888; and Elizabeth Coolidge, born on June 22, 1895. Templeman's sisters were Elizabeth Boyer ("Elise") Coolidge, born in Paris on

April 15, 1853, and married to Dr. Richard John Hall in 1879, and Roge (originally "Louise Riche"), born February 5, 1857 and married to Dr. William Duncan McKim in 1882. The Halls built the cottage behind the Coolidge barn, while the McKims converted a barn directly east of the Mansion into a cottage which became known as "The Hennery" (and later built a cottage, now gone, on Odiorne Point); Mrs. McKim died in 1895. The Hennery can be seen from the Mansion grounds. Katherine Parkman died February 13, 1900, and Templeman was married to Mary Abigail ("Gail") Parsons of Kennebunk, Maine, September 3, 1913. Templeman and Gail had two sons, Henry and Usher. Templeman died in 1945 at the age of 89. In 1954, Gail gave the Mansion to the State of New Hampshire; she died a decade later. In a gesture to history, once a year the New Hampshire Governor's Executive Council meets in the Council Chamber, the room where John Forbes Perkins and Molly were married and the setting for Henry Wadsworth Longfellow's poem, "Lady Wentworth." Molly's book has become a small, yet significant, part of that history.

Note: Genealogical information from Mrs. Malcolm Perkins and from Emma Downing Coolidge, *Descendants of John and Mary Coolidge of Watertown, Massachusetts, 1630* (Boston: Wright and Potter Printing Co., 1930), p.388; and M.A. DeWolfe Howe, *Barrett Wendell and his Letters* (Boston: Atlantic Monthly Press, 1924), p.46.

Woodard D. Openo
Somersworth, NH
October 16, 1999

Once I Was Very Young

by

MARY COOLIDGE PERKINS

MILTON · MASSACHUSETTS

1960

Printed by Thomas Todd Company
Boston, Massachusetts

Dedication

" Some adventures of my childhood "
for my Grandchildren

———

Mary Coolidge Perkins
Katharine Perkins
John Forbes Perkins 3rd

———

Malcolm Donald Perkins, Jr.
Sara Delano Perkins
Samuel Perkins
William Handasyd Perkins

———

With love
from Grandma

Chapter I

" THE BOX "

WHEN I was five we returned from Paris and my father bought a big old house on the Piscataqua River. It had belonged to a Colonial Governor of New Hampshire who had added to the original farmhouse a long ell that reached down nearly to the river and contained a billiard room, a council chamber and two card rooms, all of which were wonderful playgrounds, as were the fields, the rocks and the pine woods.

Katrine was too little to do much more than play about near the house, watched by our mother or the woman who was more of a chambermaid than a nurse. My great joy was the shore where I never tired of seeing the tide rise up and up over the pebbly beach, and where I built little walls that held it back till it rose and filled my pond on the upper side.

One morning I dropped all this at the most crucial moment, for, on looking up, I saw something that was so devastatingly exciting I could hardly breathe. On the far side of the river was a lovely island, and on its shore was a huge beautiful light-colored box, over the edge of which I could just make out the straw-colored hair and pink face of a tiny little girl about my size. She was sitting in the box clutching the edges with both hands, and Joy O Joy the box was moving — the water was holding it up. On the shore, running beside the box, were two little boys, and when the box went too far they pulled it in with a rope — then pushed it out again.

This was too much to bear alone and I rushed to the house to find my parents. My mother was far away in the garden and I ran to the nursery where my father was painting the floor.

We always talked French in those days but I will use it only occasionally.

" O, Papa," I screamed. " Viens vite, vite, sur la mer il y a une toute petite fille dans une grande boîte, et ça flotte — ça flotte." My father told me later that he pictured a child lying flat like a doll in a shoe box, and he put his paint brush into the can, took my hand and we ran down the front stairs through the living room, down the half flight through the gun room to the council chamber — through the billiard room to that window that was so near the river. And the lovely box was still floating on the very blue water, its sides flashing light in the sunshine.

" Regardes," I said. " Vois-tu — ça marche sur l'eau."

" Yes, but that child must be awfully uncomfortable. She is cramped and can hardly see over the edge," said my father. But I knew that she was the luckiest little girl in the world.

For the next three days I didn't do much but watch for the box which only came out for one short trip. On the third day I was in the corner of the living room where my parents had not seen me, and I heard my mother say, " She is eating her heart out for a box like that. Couldn't we fix that case the ice chest came in? "

" That box over there is a dangerous thing," said my father. " It leaks and there is no control whatever. Molly should have a boat." Then he saw me crying in the corner and said, " Come here, Molly, we have a wonderful idea. I think Bert Treffethan and I can build you a little row boat in about two days."

Bert was a boy who worked for my father, helping him to paint, to stop the leaks, and to make the many repairs demanded by the Wentworth Mansion. I was too little to appreciate what a sacrifice leaving this necessary work entailed, and I said, " Oui, Papa."

That evening he and Bert made drawings to show just how the boards should be cut, and next morning we three drove to the lumber yard in the beach wagon with the back seat removed.

The head man knew Bert and Papa, and was very interested in the boat, which was to have a point at one end, go straight across at the other, and have one seat in the middle. Boards cut just so for this were put in the back of the carriage, after being explained to me, who didn't much take it all in. As we were leaving, the man brought out a tiny oar. " Fisherman found it overboard," he said, " being only one it's no good to him. I'll make you the mate, and the blacksmith will make you two little oarlocks and you'll be all set, eh? " And he patted my head, much to my embarrassment.

And in two days the little boat was finished — all but the paint. I wanted it to be left its original bare pine — light like that box, but it needed protection, and we compromised on varnish outside and dark cream paint inside. When it was dry Bert and Papa carried it to the float and put it in the water, and were delighted in the morning that she hadn't leaked a drop, and that I could be put on the little seat, my back to the pointed bow, the tiny oars in my hands. Bert threw in the rope and pushed me off, and Papa was beside me in his big rowboat. He told me how to hold my hands, how to hold the water with my oars and pull against it. It worked — the boat shot ahead: once, twice, and the boat was travelling over the top of the water. My father laughed and said, " Bravo! " and I dropped an oar. He returned it to me, saying, " You do better than I expected." Full of confidence I tried again, but, after three strokes, my oar caught down very deep — below the blue water — below the green water, down, down into the blackness, something had my oar and was tipping the boat so that water was running in.

" Drop the oar, " Papa said. " That's nothing. You caught a crab, that's all, and now we'll bail out," and he gave me a sponge and used a can himself. I squeezed the sponge and dropped it overboard and it sank. I watched it spiral down down down, deeper than anything can go. " That doesn't matter, we have more sponges."

"It was not a crab," I said. "A terrible huge creature lives way down and grabbed my oar and tried to tip me over and he's got the sponge." Papa explained that catching a crab simply meant that the top edge of the oar got tipped and caught the water going in the opposite direction, and that forced it down, but I knew better. It just happened that my father had never met up with that monster, and I had. He saw that I was still troubled and suggested our towing my boat, while I sat on the seat beside him and rowed one of my oars instead of two. That went well. His work on the Mansion was neglected each morning for an hour while he rowed beside me, and I was soon enjoying the speed and ease with which I was skimming over the waters of that beautiful bay and river.

One morning Papa said, "How would you like it if I stayed on the float today instead of rowing beside you? Mama is coming, and I have three friends who want to see your boat." I liked it, and the gentlemen came with Mama and admired the boat and pushed me off. I rowed as far as the end of the island till Papa called through the megaphone for me to turn slowly, and pass close to the float as Mr. Deland had a camera. As I passed, the gentlemen were laughing and one said, "Tiny boat — tiny girl — congratulations, Templeman," which didn't make sense as I was doing the rowing. When I landed I did not hit the float with my bow or with my oar, and they said, "Bravo," and Mr. Deland took the painter and dropped two loops over the post, just right, so that I did not have that job to do, and gave me his hand to help me hop up onto the high float. He smiled at me so pleasantly that I wanted to tell him something.

"Vois-tu cette île là-bas?" I said. "Dans cette maison il y a une toute petite fille. Elle a une tres grande boîte — and that box is like magic, it floats right on top of the water with the little girl inside. It doesn't touch the stones — the water pushes it right up and it floats, and moves along."

"Well, well, imagine that," said the gentlemen, but my father

[4]

was shaking his head in a puzzled way. " That box," he mut-
tered. I took his hand and we walked happily up the steep gangplank, back to the house.

Eddie was about ten and lived on the island with the Mulloons,
though he was not one of the family. He said he had no last
name. He used to row over each morning with milk, and sometimes eggs or berries. He had never spoken to me or I to him,
but one morning I was in the kitchen when he came in, and I
mustered all my courage to ask an answer to a very burning
question. In my excitement I forgot that he couldn't understand, and I started in with, " Je ne vois pas la boîte sur la plage
— jamais, jamais."

" Don't she talk funny? " said Eddie to the cook.

" Tell him English, dearie," said the cook. " You stay where
y' are Eddie."

" Where is the beautiful big box that used to be on your shore?
The water pushed it from under and it floated. I never see it,"
I gasped in one breath.

" Kindling wood," said Eddie. " It was this way. Sadie, she is
lightest, and it sank with any one but her, so we put her in it
and pushed her out and hauled her back with the rope. First
time she didn't mind, but being cramped and wet, she wouldn't
go again; we had to force her in and she got awful wet and
mucked up with the paint and putty we tried to stop them
leaks with."

" The last day Pa Mulloon, he heard Sadie hollerin', and
found we was scrunching her up and forcing her into the box,
hoping to push it farther than ever before, but it hadn't gone
beyond the rock before Pa was on us with a stick, and did he
lambaste us! He walked into the water and untangled Sadie
where she was rolled up, and then and there he chopped that box
to bits and it's behind the kitchen stove.

[5]

"We watches you outa window," he continued. "That's a elegant boat. Pa says you rows good," and with that Eddie dashed to the door, refusing a piece of cake.

I rushed into the living room where my mother and father were sitting by the fire with Katrine, and threw myself into my mother's arms.

"It's kindling wood — it's burning up — that box is gone," I sobbed. "They scrunched the little girl all up into a small piece so they could force her in, and she hated it and screamed and got all paint and putty."

Mama hugged me. Papa showed me some kindling that came from a big box that had held the ice chest, and said that was the best use for boxes like that. If people tried to go boating in them it only ended in difficulties and danger.

I went to bed that night feeling older than my six years. Tragedy had entered my life. One beautiful dream had gone, but a new one had come. I had done as well as my father hoped I would when the company came down to the float. All that difficult part about the oars and catching crabs, and looping ropes, and making landings had been overcome, or nearly so, and I dropped off dreaming that I was rowing alone all the way around the island, the moon making a path on the water, and a glow on my own little tiny "elegant" boat, and Eddie had said I "rowed good."

Next day my mother and I rowed over to the island with a new pink dress for Sadie.

Chapter II

THE TINY SAILBOAT

For several years I continued to row about in my tiny boat, the only out being that it was so small that someone must watch me from the float or from another boat. I also often sailed with my father in his large catboat; I could handle the tiller unless it blew very hard, but I was not strong enough to hoist the sail or to pull it in.

One day my father said, " Molly, I think you understand pretty well how to get the sail to catch the wind in the right way and you have been making very good landings, but this boat is too heavy for you. How would you like to have a little, small sailboat of your own, a catboat like this, but very small? " This was too much to grasp and I said there wasn't any such thing. My father went on to say that he knew of a man on Cape Cod who built lovely catboats, and that he might build us one as small as we wished. This was more than I could take in as a reality, and I was floating on clouds for two days. On the third my father and I took the train to Boston and there changed stations for Osterville, where we were driven to Mr. Crosby's boat yard, which seemed a very confusing place to me, as everyone was sawing and planing on what were only pieces of boats. Mr. Crosby led us to a nearly finished one saying, " That's a good model." My father said it was much too big and told Mr. Crosby he had brought me along to scale the new boat by. " Well, well," said Mr. Crosby, staring at me as though I were rather unsatisfactory. " You going to sail this new boat all alone by yourself?" " Of course," I said, with all the scorn I could muster. He glared at me again, asked my weight and scrawled something on a bit of paper. " No more than nine foot overall," he said;

"fairly high on water, decked over all around, and about six foot wide; centreboard and plenty of ballast will allow her a pretty big sail. In two days I'll mail you a little model." They talked some more, but I didn't understand and was getting hungry; and we had milk and sandwiches and drove back to the station. On the Portsmouth train I was carsick and forgot about the boat. It remained rather vague, but in four days a package about a foot and a half long arrived in the mail. It contained a board to which was fastened the model of one half a boat, slit down through the middle. "Working model of your boat, Molly." "Oh, won't it have two sides?" I moaned, but I soon understood, and the board was hung in my bedroom, though nothing seemed real as yet. After two months of normal living, word came from the city that there were a boat and spars in a bundle at the freight office, and with some difficulty arrangements were made for delivery. On a day of sunshine a wonderful sight appeared on the water road that led to the landing. On a big flat dray dragged by two horses sat upright the most beautiful little white boat with shiny varnished decks. The varnished mast and spars lay in the dray and extended far out behind. The bundle held the sails. "Is that my own boat?" "It is," my father said, while he and Cyrus and the expressman planned how to get her off the wagon and onto the tracks that led over the beach into the water. After what seemed a long struggle, the little boat was floating and moored to the dock. After lunch the mast was stepped with its boom and gaff and rigging, and the little sail was laced on. My father asked whether I preferred to have him with me on the first trip or would I go alone. "All alone," and they pushed me off and the wind caught my sail. There couldn't be a more fortunate or a happier girl in the world. The ease with which I could let the sail all the way out, then head up and pull it in without effort was a revelation after my father's heavy sail; and the way she skimmed over the water was a dream too good to be true. As I turned and passed the float again my father called to me to go before the wind again and pull up the centreboard. As it had some ballast it was a little heavy, but I could handle it.

For the next two days I was coached from the float about landings without catching the board on the outhaul ropes, or the main sheet on the posts. It was difficult to follow these directions, but after a few days Papa told me I was on my own, but must always tell him where I was going. I used to go around the island and up the creek, and always it was a great adventure.

In wintertime I went to Miss Fiske's school. She was a friend of my mother's and was coming to visit us. My mother told me she had a boat of her own and was a wonderful swimmer and sailor and, if I would invite her, she might love to have a sail with me. She arrived on a lovely day and I lost no time with the invitation. It was settled that we should go right after lunch, as there was a good breeze and the tide would be high.

After lunch I went down to make sure that the boat was alongside and clean and bailed out nicely, and saw my father and mother and Miss Fiske walking down the dock. My passenger-to-be had on a bright red dress, a large shade hat from which hung a white veil, and on her hands were white gloves. I must have looked startled, for she said that she burned dreadfully and had to cover up like this, — " but it leaves me free as air, and I can carry out any orders you care to give me," she laughed. As I had hoisted the sail, the boom was in her way, and she did just what she would have done in her own catboat. She grasped the mast and stepped on the forward deck, ready to swing around into the cockpit. There was an awful jerk and sideways lurch — I jumped to the upper side, but to no avail. My boat was going over. But Miss Fiske had jumped and was down under water beyond us. Horrified, I watched the eddy where she had disappeared; first to rise were the red flowers on her hat, then her hat and her veil-covered face. Her white-gloved hands were pushing the veil up from her face — just as though she were arranging herself in a mirror, I thought. She had stopped treading water and was striking out for the float, but Cyrus and my mother and father could not pull her up, and she swam to shore and walked to the house, leaving a trail of red dye all the way.

She was a wonderful sport and laughed about it all, especially over the picture of herself poking up the veil with her white gloves. " You were wonderfully clearheaded to jump so quickly," said my father. " There was no point in sinking Molly and her boat as well as myself," she laughed.

She returned to Boston and soon married Dr. B., Head of Harvard Medical School. Two of her three sons were varsity football players and one became Governor of Massachusetts, and so her courage carries on.

WATERSIDE OF WENTWORTH MANSION

MOLLY — 6 YRS.

MOLLY — 11 YRS.

Chapter III

THE CIRCUS

KATRINE and I had been taken to a circus in a field next the cemetery. It was a very small affair with one tent, two horses, an elephant and a lion, some acrobats and a clown; but we thought it was the most wonderful thing we'd ever seen, and we soon decided to give a circus of our own. Beyond the barn was an open field with a good bit of flat land. On one side stood two large apple trees one of which already had a rope hanging from an upper branch. This was a good start, as we were good at shinning up it, but it was the only start we had in mind. Next time B. Wendell came over we asked him to be in the circus and he said, " Goat race — I'll put mine with its sulky in the boat and row it over. Where'll we make a ring? " We showed him the field, and as there was some cut hay left about, we used it for the edges of a large ring that circled both apple trees. " Be back a week from Saturday with goat and family, show at three o'clock," said B. and that was that.

There were now four of us and our parents were tremendously occupied with us and the big house and place and all, so we decided to have the circus a surprise. " But then there'd be no audience," I said, so we told them that a week from Saturday at three P.M. there would be a circus and they could supply the audience, not a huge one, more of a family audience. Next day Cyrus put up another rope in the second apple tree and we practised a little each day.

As to costumes, Jennie, our nurse, said she would help. I wanted to be ringmaster and Jennie dyed my long winter under-wear a bright red; my rubber boots and Papa's old top hat would do the rest. Katrine wanted to be a clown — an old pair of bloomers with the knee elastic removed, a mask and a pointed cap would do that. Louise wanted to be a fairy, but I told her there were no fairies in circuses, but she could be a beautiful fluffy equestrienne and lead the horse in the parade; but Louise was really too little for this and refused, and we settled that she was to drag Jack at the end of the parade in his own little cart and I would lead the parade snapping my whip, but then who could drive our goat, as Katrine wanted to enter on the family horse, beating her little drum while we all sang " Onward Christian Soldiers "?

" We've got a week to settle it in," I said, and we went to lunch. Katrine was late and my mother went to look for her. She came back laughing. " She is washing up now," she said. " I found her in Gypsy's stall sitting on her back beating the drum." " Rehearsing," I said, " so Gypsy won't be scared."

Cyrus added to the hay that formed the ring, and beyond it he drove in three stakes that held up a long canvas that had been covering boats; this was to be our dressing room and our hiding place before the parade started.

The great day arrived, sunny and beautiful. Jennie, the cook, and Cyrus had carried up all the kitchen and bedroom chairs and all the outside benches and boat cushions for our own household; the Careys, Uncle Duncan and Aunt Rogé, Gerty Hyde's grandmother, mother and aunt, and several Sturgises were all coming. From two on we watched the ocean as we made final costume arrangements and at 2.30 B. W. landed his cargo on our beach. The sulky was in the stern seat hanging out over the water. The central seat had been removed and on the bottom lay the goat with Mary Wendell, B.'s sister, sitting on its head. B. was rowing in the bow seat. " O," groaned Mary, " that was so awful. Can I get up? " " Wait," said B. " He'll break his legs getting out — wanting to jump all the way over; you hold one horn, I've got the other." They eased out a very furious goat and led him to the back of the canvas where our goat was already hidden. Katrine was arriving on the carriage horse, who had on three feathers from the duster fastened with adhesive and standing up straight from the bridle. She had on her clown's outfit, an old piece of red velvet under her and the drum in one hand.

Soon Cyrus came to speak to us. "Your Pa says folks is all come," he said; and I swaggered up to the audience and said, "The show will now commence," snapping my whip, from which I never could get a sound. Katrine appeared from behind the canvas and I ran back to jump into the goat cart to follow. When nearing the audience, Katrine started the little drum, and the feathers flopped down over Gypsy's right eye. With a lumbering motion she was over the edge of the ring and off into the field, my goat after her. I was able to bring her back, and B., who had been following, said, "The others are back of canvas; you tell the audience that was an extra; you tell them the show hasn't started yet." "You do," I said. "No." It was a chance to be ringmaster and snap my whip, which I couldn't do in the goatcart and I remembered the coaching Uncle Joe had given me about speaking loud and clear when play acting. "Ladies and Gentlemen," I shouted, "that was just an extra, the real show will start in one minute." Laughter and great applause.

Katrine was slowly returning minus the feathers, the drum, and her mask. "Didn't like the drum after all," said Katrine unperturbed. Cyrus was holding my goat and I ran back to tell those behind the canvas that we'd start where we were and they were to follow any old way. Katrine and Gypsy started off, Gypsy's head hanging very low. The two goat carts followed and after quite a gap came Gertie Hyde with her little cocker spaniel who was fitted to a harness and dragging a tiny carriage. G.'s grandmother had dressed her in a lovely early American dress with a lace bonnet, and she walked behind the carriage guiding the dog with long reins. Great applause. Louise was to follow in her fluffy ruffles leading our St. Bernard dog. She was good with dogs and we hoped that Jack would sit on Barney's back as a cupid, but he always slipped off with a smile and demanded his shirt back. Louise now followed Gerty with Barney at her side, and as she passed the audience the dog left her to lie on my father's feet, and she continued alone. By now I had circled the ring and reached the canvas and retrieved Jack, who was starting off down the field, and dragged him in his little cart halfway around the ring when he slipped off, found the audience, and sat in my mother's lap.

Behind the canvas Cyrus was leading the horse back to its stall and B. was holding both goats. Katrine had on a little boy's blue bathing suit and I dropped my long drawers, rubber boots and jacket, to appear in a bright red bathing suit. I announced that the great aerialists Orlando and Orlandia had arrived from Europe to do their act, and we walked to the ropes. She went half-way up hers and I three-quarters-way up mine and we swung till I could reach her rope and cross over and slide down till she reached the ground and ran to my rope. We did this twice and the third time each climbed to the top of her rope to sit on the branch of the apple tree while Cyrus tied the ropes together. I came down my side to hang by my legs in the loop till Katrine came down and sat in my arms. Her feet were only a foot from the ground but it seemed to us that we might well be near the top of a high tent. I dropped her amidst great applause and we ran close to the audience and stood on our heads holding tightly to the grass for balance. Next Gerty appeared again with her dog — took him out of his harness and he performed some pleasant tricks. Then, having forgotten my ringleader costume, I made another announcement.

"Ladies and Gentlemen, the grand finale has arrived; the great goat trainer, Mr. B. Wendell, is to race his goat against that terrific creature, the Coolidge goat," and I ran back to get onto the sulky. "Gotta start even," growled B., and Cyrus stood between the goats, holding their heads. We were both beating our goats till Cyrus saw that they were even and jumped to one side. We were on the dead run and, wonderful to relate, we stayed inside the ring for two rounds, when Mr. Wendell announced that Coolidge goat was winner by three inches. We started the next race where we were, and after twice around Mr. W. announced that Wendell goat was by three inches the winner, and that the last race would settle it. We beat our goats. They galloped madly, and as we approached the final chair I felt that I might be an inch behind and with a shout I lashed out. My goat leaped forward and a bit to one side. There was an awful crash and I fell off my seat — our wheels were locked. I was unhurt but angry, and B. was growling, " All your fault." Mr. Wendell was speaking, " We have witnessed three beautiful, exciting races and we can now announce that the goats are equally victorious, there has been no winner, the result of the races is a tie."

Cyrus handed a box of raspberries to my father, who stepped forward. " This was to have been the prize for the winner," said my father, " and it is going to a very brave young lady who, in the bottom of the boat all the way from Newcastle, prevented this brute from jumping overboard by sitting on his head — Miss Mary Wendell," and he handed her the box amidst great applause. She smiled very happily, and the show was over.

Chapter IV

A GOAT AND A PLAY

WHEN I was nearing eight Joe Smith came into our lives bringing endless adventure in the form of expeditions and plays. As he lived near the Carey pine woods, the first play was to be there in a clearing with pine trees, rocks and moss as background. Katrine and I were to be King and Queen of the fairies, and Mrs. Jack Gardner was coming on the train from Boson to see the play and was spending the night at our house. This meant that there was more sprucing up than usual in progress; everything must be clean and neat. Papa was fixing up the beachwagon in which he would meet Mrs. Gardner at the train. He and Cyrus washed and combed the fringe around the top that covered the carriage, polished the harness and its brasses, and even washed the horse's mane and tail. Next day Papa put on his tweed jacket and straw hat and drove to Portsmouth.

We had a large goat with branching horns, a good harness and a varnished racing sulky. He was a wonderful goat, as he butted everyone but me and Katrine, and was capable of tremendous speed when headed homeward. Making any progress away from home took endless urgings and beatings, and I had never had the patience to go more than three-quarters of a mile even for the reward of that race home. On this same morning Katrine had determined to urge the goat all the way to Portsmouth, and she did it. She wanted to buy something.

As my father was driving Mrs. Gardner through town, homeward bound, everything fine and dandy, she grabbed his arm, " Templeman, just look at that extraordinary child." The goat was on the dead run, passing the carriage, Katrine was leaning forward, her bare feet in metal supports on the shafts, her long light hair, loose from its ribbon, streamed over her face, and there had been a puddle which had left its mark of mud on goat and child. My father was amazed and could hardly believe his eyes, as he had never imagined the goat or Katrine so far from home. " That," he said, " is my daughter."

The goat arrived at the Mansion just behind the carriage, and Mrs. Gardner took a step toward the sulky. " If you move a bit nearer she'll butt her horns right through you," said Katrine. My mother, who had come out to greet her guest, took one startled look at Katrine and said, " Well, if you are to be queen of the fairies this afternoon, better come in for a good bath and shampoo."

Mrs. Gardner was delighted by the look of the shore and the sea and wanted to see the boats and boathouse, which were just what my father wanted to show her. She said my boat was a beauty. " I'm dreadfully afraid of boats," she said, " but I long to step right into this one." " If you put one foot in," I said, " you'll go right down to the very bottom." " Gracious, Templeman," she laughed, " your daughters make me feel in constant danger."

After lunch she ran up to her room to bring down the dress she planned to wear to the play. " You can see how the green and brown changeable silk blouse harmonizes with the woods," she said, " and the belt," and from her handbag came a long string of flashing lights. " The emeralds and diamonds are for the pine trees also." They were dazzling, but I knew that Mrs. Smith had, in her costume trunk, something just as beautiful for me and Katrine.

We had a nap, and Cyrus drove us to the Smiths' house, to go back later for the others. We had our own white dresses on for underpinnings and it was fun to see the brilliant gauzes, velvets and brocades that were to go over them. Mine was a purple velvet cape with gold flowers embroidered on it, and I had a sceptre and a golden crown; and Katrine's was a salmony pink velvet cape and a crown of pink roses. Mr. Smith, Sr., was as clever at complicated scenery as his wife was at costumes, and we knew that we were to be hidden by a screen of cedars that would fall at the right moment, but this could not be rehearsed. We had not seen the arrangement till Joe told us to come to the woods and climb the stepladder behind our thrones to a board that led to two little seats; then we realized that we were each in the heart of a huge poppy six feet across, mine pink, Katrine's lavender. Something magic seemed to be happening.

" Some of the audience is beginning to arrive," said Joe, " and the fairies are coming in behind you as fast as mother gets them dressed. Are you comfortable enough to stay quiet right where you are for a while? I can't have you getting mussed up." Then he said to the fairies who were hiding behind us, " Anyone who moves about or makes a sound will be sent back to the house. The people on the other side of the screen are not to know there is a soul in these woods."

There was a crack in the poppy behind my ear and Mrs. Smith was on the stepladder. She whispered to me that Joe was about to enter on the far side of the screen, which would fall after he had talked a while, and she was right there to tell me when to speak. This was comforting and soon I heard Joe singing and telling in verse that he was lost in the forest and could find no food. I knew that he was dressed in a sort of Howard Pyle's Robin Hood jerkin and cap and carried a guitar on which he strummed, making an appeal to the little people, if they existed, to help an exhausted, starving soul. " Don't be startled," whispered Mrs. Smith. " The trees are going to fall and then you will speak." They fell and I *was* startled, not by the fall but by a sea of white faces so near, and staring at us. There was a prolonged clatter of applause which gave Mrs. Smith the opportunity to tell me to speak very loud and how to start. This had been well rehearsed and, in verse, I asked the poor man how the little people could help him. He told of his troubles, and then came Katrine's turn. I looked at her and she was perfectly lovely, sitting in the center of that huge poppy, her long light hair hanging from under the rose crown over her velvet cape, and she was smiling happily at each friend in the audience. "Katrine can't speak," said Mrs. Smith. "You go on and send for the fairies." I repeated the familiar lines, whereupon all the smallest neighboring children dashed in from behind our thrones, the girls in fluffy gauze of light shades, the boys in green and brown elfin suits. Four of these were carrying a huge melon for Joe, from which he ate and drank, and recovered in a most rapid manner. He strummed on his guitar, singing, "Yo ho for the melon, the beautiful melon, that merrily bursts apart. Yo ho for the wine that grows on the vine to cheer the sinking heart," and all the while the fairies were dancing about, bringing branches to make Joe more comfortable, bringing grapes and berries for him to eat. He stood up to thank the King and Queen and the fairies, and the elves helped him along and showed him a secret, hidden way out of the forest. He walked around back and lifted me and Katrine out of our poppies and took us into the midst of the people.

"Joe," said Mrs. Gardner, "that was so beautiful I can't get my breath." "You will," said Joe; "and that dress of yours should have been on the stage." "I knew that," she said, "and I wanted to take it off to give it to you; and you did well," she said to me and to Katrine, but we knew that the hit of the piece had been the poppies.

Chapter V

WANDERING MINSTRELS

THE following year, four friends came to visit and we decided to be wandering minstrels. Katrine and Sophy had violins and played well, and we had all learned carols, madrigals, and old English songs at the Bennetts.

We gained permission to take the family horse and the old wagon that was used on the place. We asked Cyrus not to clean the horse and to give us the shabbiest-looking harness he could assemble. As to our get-ups, the maids cooperated with cast-off aprons and skirts, which they shortened up. We had handkerchiefs for our heads and didn't brush our hair or wash for two days. As we went barefoot always, our feet and legs were dark with sunburn and were genuinely scratched by brambles and rocks, our faces and arms being equally brown; and we really were justified in feeling that we looked like very poor country children. The great day came and we sallied forth armed with two violins and some bread.

Our first objective was to be the Wentworth Hotel, three miles away, and beyond that were many summer cottages, too far for anyone to recognize us. As we approached the hotel, we decided to tie the horse to a tree at the foot of the hill and walk the rest of the way. We would look poorer without a horse, and it would be hard to hold him while we sang. As we passed a simple cottage, we decided to sing here as a practise before trying the hotel, and we burst into " Since first I saw your face." It was going well when a woman in a wrapper, a mop in her hand, burst open the door. " You get out of here," she screamed. " I seen that hoss in the city and I know you're rich folks disturbing the poor and trying to get their money. Get along," and she rushed at us with her mop. We walked on up the hill, feeling rather frightened and depressed by our first attempt; anyway no one else need see the horse.

At the hotel, a large group of men were seated with newspapers on a long piazza that fronted on the road, and we stood below and rather tremulously started on our repertoire. There was loud applause, and after a few songs three of the gentlemen came down to talk to us, bringing a good many quarters from the others. One of them asked to see Katrine's violin, an Amati that Martin Loeffler had found for her. He asked about it, and Katrine said it was a " hairloom " in the family. " If your family ever want to sell it I could give you a good price." " No," said Katrine. " You tell them about this, and I'll give you my name," and he told us that he and his friends were violins in the Boston Symphony Orchestra, and in summertime played evenings at the hotel. He gave Katrine his name on a paper which she put in her pocket and then he startled us by asking for her name. We had not thought up any names, so there was a pause. " Her name is Mabel Chick," I said, " and we have walked all the way from Hampton." "Address," said the man. " C/o Henry Chick, Hampton." " Street? " " No street," I said.

We felt urged to move along and proceeded on our way, enriched by more quarters than we could have hoped for. Out of sight of the hotel we gasped with relief and sat on the bank to eat some of our dry bread. " That about names — that was a close one."

As we moved on we chose the most prosperous cottages, remembering our first tragic effort, and we sang our songs to moderate enthusiasm and rather scant reward; but it was more than we had hoped for at the start. The hotel musicians had raised our standard too high. We thought it might be time to turn back, but ahead of us was a lovely white house with big shade trees and a green lawn, and we decided to try that as the last effort. As we approached we saw that two gentlemen were rolling balls on the lawn, and we started right in with our music before they would interrupt us. We sang four songs while they sat on the grass and clapped, and when we came to " Since first I saw your face," they jumped up and joined us. With their tenor and bass, the two violins, and our voices, we felt it to be simply wonderful and were having a perfect time. The gentlemen wanted it all over again, and then asked for that " Wassail Song " we had done at the start, and they could sing with us again. The words went as follows: " We are not daily beggars who beg from door to door. But we are neighbor's children whom you have seen before. Love and joy come to you and to you your Wassail true, and God bless you and bring you a Happy New Year," etc. The two gentlemen laughed and each gave us fifty cents while a maid brought milk from the house. While we drank avidly, the tall gentleman said, " Have you ever been to Little Harbor? " I was on the point of saying No, but the training of my youth interfered and I murmured " Yes." " Well you go on over there, and go to the Wentworth Mansion, for I am sure that my friend Mr. Coolidge would enjoy your music, and you tell him that Benson and Tarbell send their greetings." " Yes," we murmured and we thanked them and said Goodbye.

" My, wonder how they knew us. Too bad they did, but they were so nice it didn't matter," was the burden of our conversation as we walked back. As we approached the hotel Mr. Swan, the first violin, was on a chair on the lawn watching out for us. He wanted some more conversation about that violin, and walked along with us. As we neared the cross lady's house we told him about her and he offered to go in and scold her. " No, no," we cried, terrified over the idea of her disclosing us as frauds, but now we were approaching our horse.

This was awful, as it had been definite that we had walked from Hampton. A whisper travelled from one to the other, " Pass the horse, pass on," and on we walked, fearing that Mr.

Swan would never turn back. He finally did, and Gypsy, who had been getting very impatient, outdid herself in speeding home.

We told all our adventures and poured what seemed untold wealth of quarters and fifty-cent pieces out onto the table, and gave the messages from Mr. Benson and Mr. Tarbell. "I'm glad they knew you," said Papa. "I think they are the very best artists painting today."

Two years later there was a pleasant sequel to our adventure. A mutual friend brought Mr. Swan to dinner and we told him the whole story. He seemed bewildered, as we had grown apace and were nicely dressed, till we showed him the violin, and he said, "Now I believe you," and he laughed and laughed, saying this was the best thing he had ever heard. He said that he and the other musicians had not had the slightest doubt about our being the country children we claimed to be, who had walked from Hampton and who had the "hairloom violin". When we came to our having to pass our horse on his account he almost went under the table. "Best thing I ever heard of," he repeated; "and now, can we hear that violin again?"

Chapter VI

HORSES

WHEN we were six and seven Mama used to hire a horse one day a week and go riding on a side saddle, while Katrine and I waited on the grass on the side of the avenue for her to return. Then, joy of joys, the side saddle would come off, to leave a blanket pad which we straddled, to walk up and down, and gradually to trot. As I was a year and a half older, I felt superior in every way, and could hardly believe it when Katrine trotted faster and longer than I could. She was always better with horses. With a new baby and too much to do, our mother stopped hiring the horse, and some years went by before we rode again.

Six years later, on my first visit to West Medford, Esther and Sue Hallowell and Ruth Bennett were galloping bareback on a pony, and asked me if I could ride. " O yes," I said, thinking about Mama's hired horse. I pulled myself up by the pony's mane, and he started off to curve the field on the dead run. " Lean, lean," called the girls, and I leaned out, away from the centre of the circle, and landed on my head. As Browny was not a tall pony I was ready to try again and this time I leaned inward and circled many times, and pulled up triumphantly in front of the others, feeling there was nothing like riding and that I was pretty good at it.

" You are hauling on his mouth," said Ruth. " You've got to think about the horse, but you've got guts, if nothing else." She had a horse named " Kitty " who was forty years old and single stepped most of the time. Ruth taught us all the finer points of horsemanship on Kitty, who lived on for many years.

The following summer our neighbor Mr. Arthur Carey, whom I adored, gave us his polo pony, for which he had grown too heavy, and Katrine and I went for long rides every day.

Diamond had one bad trick of rearing when she was frightened, instead of shying to one side as most horses do. One day I came out of a wood road into a field where a horsedrawn rake was clattering and clanking. Diamond took fright and stood up straight on her hind legs and, to my amazement, went over crash onto her back. I subconsciously jumped clear, and she went across the field to eat grass. The English saddle and I were slightly bruised, and I rode home to tell Katrine about it.

" That was entirely your own fault," she said. " You know that Diamond wouldn't want to fall on her back — you pulled on her mouth when she reared, and you made her do it. She might have been hurt. You should have given her a loose rein and touched her with the crop and she would have jumped ahead; you do that next time she rears." By silent agreement we never mentioned Diamond's rearing to the family.

The following winter Katrine was also old enough to be invited to West Medford, where dear Aunt Sally Hallowell and the Colonel opened their warm arms to us, giving us a second home and the happiest times that any young people could have. All our school vacations were spent there, or in our third home with the Bennetts in Wayland.

Ruth found an immediate and understanding ally in Katrine, who could understand horse mentality. I loved to ride and to go on driving picnics, but did not feel too enthusiastic about studying the horse's psychology, or washing his tail, as Ruth and Katrine and Sue Hallowell all did. They would spend hours fitting together bits of harness, and drove miles and miles to all the livery stables till they found an old pole with which to drive a pair. There were blacksmiths and harness-makers in those days and we soon had the pole attached to the carriage with two whiffletrees for the traces. Ruth was an enthusiast on the lightest possible harness, and the collars were put away to be replaced by light breastplates with long traces.

Three saddle ponies and another carriage horse had been

brought from Wayland, and we were ready for our wonderful all-day picnics in the Middlesex Fells, at that time a series of wild woods and ponds.

We used to go to the firehouse to see the quick harnessing of the horses, and Ruth soon decided that our harness should drop from above, so we spent a rainy day rigging it in the ceiling of the barn. It used to startle the horses, falling in rather a pile that had to be straightened out. I thought that we got off more quickly when taking the harness off its usual hook on the wall, especially as I was the one who had to go up on the roof beams.

The public school was near by, and to avoid a slow corner we used to cut across the schoolyard on the gallop, to come out on the main road. We took great pride in the hundreds of eager faces at the schoolhouse windows, but the principal of the school came to call on Mrs. Hallowell, to say that when we galloped through, ringing our bell, every child in the building left its desk to rush to the windows; so from then on we had to trot slowly around the corner.

We did not get to many fires, as we were too often in the far woods when an alarm came, but once we reached a brush fire ahead of the department and we put it out with brooms. The firemen never heard the end of that.

This had been before school started, and when the Easter vacation came in April, Katrine and I, with Esther and Sue Hallowell, moved to the lovely old house and the dear Bennett family in Wayland. There our horses took us to the Sudbury woods, where we saw no house, no human being, and felt far away in a wild forest wilderness. One day we came on a lovely deep pond and decided to tie up there for lunch; but first, here was a good chance to try riding bareback in our bare skins, and we galloped around and around the pond. Katrine said, " I'm a centaur, the horse's muscles and mine are all one — let's eat."

We had a swim first, but, instead of tying up my horse, I decided to see what it felt like to be on a horse while it swam.

ELIZABETH

KATRINE — I I YRS.

MOLLY   BILLY THE GOAT   KATRINE   LOUISE   JACK

The horse balked completely at the idea of going into the pond, but some whacks from behind and kicks from my heels got him in, and we soon slumped into deep water and were headed across. I was completely appalled by the angle at which a horse swims, as it felt to me as though he were sinking and struggling hard to keep up. His hindquarters seemed at a straight angle down and I crept up onto his neck. Then remembering pictures of men swimming horses across rivers, I slipped off, holding tight to his mane. That was better, as he came higher in the water, but his hoofs seemed very near. It is a strange feeling to be in bathing with a horse.

We ate our sandwiches and apples and drove home. In the evening we sang with Ned Bennett at the piano, two violins, a cello and a viola. We were indeed fortunate in having such wonderful friends, and our vacations were truly glorious.

During the winter a letter had come from Cyrus in Portsmouth stating the astonishing and startling news that Diamond had produced a colt, as a complete surprise to all. It was a black female with an elongated white diamond running between the eyes down its face. " And its name is Ruth, after Ruth Bennett," said Katrine, " and I'm the trainer."

It seemed as though the last day of school would never come, but at last, early in June, we all moved to Portsmouth, and before carrying any bags we rushed to the barn to find that the colt was all that we could have hoped for.

Next morning Patsy Shea, whose father had a farm, brought our milk, with some advice about horse training. He said that Ruth was strong enough to carry a bag of oats on her back, and we strapped it on and led her about by the halter. He found an old bridle and cut it down, saying that she'd better learn the feel of a bit, and to guide by the neck. She was too young to be ridden but the following summer Katrine rode her bareback, and, as all went well, the rides became longer and Katrine and Ruth were going pretty far from home.

One day the plumber came to fix the kitchen pump and said to Mama, " Seed your girl on the Banfield Road yesterday." " It MUST have been someone else," said Mama. " She couldn't be so far from home." " There's not such an awful lot of barefoot girls on black colts," said the man. After lunch Katrine was questioned. " It's such a lovely wild woodsy road," she said, " and Ruth loves it; it's soft on her feet," and then she told the whole story.

On the Banfield road, just on our side of Newington, there was a trotting track where Katrine had watched a man driving a green horse in a training sulky. He had stopped to ask about the colt and Katrine told how she had broken her to the saddle, but could make no headway with harness. The man suggested they try her in the sulky, and he put his horse in the shed, and shortened a few straps, and they were off, he and Katrine both on the little straw seat, legs extending over the shafts. Ruth kicked, but the length of the training shafts prevented her from reaching the drivers, and a satisfactory start was made. The man was as delighted as Katrine was, and invited her to come every day, which invitation she accepted with alacrity. She had returned twice, when Mama had to tell her that she could not ever again go so far from home on her lone rides. " That darned plumber," was her only reply.

Now, since a new way must be thought of breaking Ruth to harness, our Wayland and West Medford training stood us in good stead. We bought an old pole and with the help of the blacksmith made it interchangeable with the shafts in the family carriage. Ruth was to go double with steady old Gypsy. The training on the Banfield Road must have helped, for we travelled pretty successfully, and after a few weeks we could take Louise and Jack for drives, squeezed between us on the front seat. Ruth had inherited one bad trait from her mother, Diamond, and she reared when really frightened. A slap of the whip would keep her down until a new terror came into her life. Parallel to the graveyard a track had been laid for a horsecar, and to go either way we had to drive a half mile on the road with the track. We met the horsecar constantly, and Ruth would stand almost straight. We developed a system. As soon as we saw the car approaching, Katrine would stand at the horses' heads while I ran Louise and Jack and later Elizabeth to the graveyard wall and dropped them over. They could just see over and were safe. After a while Katrine thought that this method was not good for Ruth's training. " Next time I'm not going to hold her down. We've got to stay in the carriage." So when the horsecar came rattling, I threw the children into the graveyard and jumped into the seat beside Katrine. Ruth reared and Katrine lashed out with the whip. Ruth bucked, the horsecar clattered, and Ruth was over the pole on Gypsy's side. The driver of the car handed his reins to a passenger and came to our help. Soon all the passengers were helping, some very curious about the tiny children peering over the graveyard wall. The pole was dislodged and our pair had to be unharnessed to straighten out the tangle. " Anyway, Ruth is not hurt," said Katrine.

As the pole did not seem just right we walked our pair slowly home, and that night, with the advice of our parents, we decided that Ruth was too good a saddle horse to be forced to harness. But we must have a use for that lovely pole, and for many years Gypsy and Diamond drove us about very successfully.

Chapter VII

CAMPING ON THE ISLAND

KATRINE and I had driven to the station to meet three friends who were coming to visit, and as they jumped off the train with their bags our excitement ran high. This was their first visit and there was so much in store for them that it seemed as though something wild must be done about it. I was driving and a crazy mood was upon me. When Sue said, " How far is it? " I said, " Right here," as I turned the horse into a narrow path that led to a shabby little brown house with a roofless shed beyond. Katrine, though we had had nothing of the sort in mind, hopped out saying, " Here we are; all out, kids. Hand me your bags." The girls looked crestfallen, and one said, " Where is the ocean? " Katrine said, " Beyond that grave-yard." Then we were startled to see that an old man was seated very near us in a dark corner of the porch, half hidden by an ash can.

" Is this the Wentworth Mansion? " said Katrine. " Wentworth Mansion, Wentworth Mansion," he mumbled. " Yes — I heard tell of it." At that moment a woman dashed out, and I said, " Could you please direct us to the Wentworth Mansion? " " I'll Wentworth Mansion you," she shouted. " Don't I know thet hoss and carriage? " By this time the bags and girls were back in their places and we turned to drive down through the white pines and high boulders of the Little Harbor Road. At the end we stopped between two stone posts and looked down at the beautiful old house, pale yellow against the very blue sea, its long ell set off by the gnarled lilac bushes at one end and the huge apple tree at the other. " That's too big," said one. " Now see here," said another; " we've come a long trip to get here, and we don't want any more of your tricks; you take us home this time." We drove silently and slowly down the avenue, past the huge wooded rock on one side, the sea on the other, and as we drove over the crunchy sea gravel at the front door, Mama and Papa came out to greet our friends and they knew that this time it was home.

We went to bed early that night because we had a plan. Katrine and I had two small bedrooms opening into each other. They used to be dressing rooms for the Governor, and Katrine's had a large window opening out to the roof of the billiard room ell. Our friends' rooms could, without going through the main hall, be reached by a secret passage that was a part of the old attic. We showed them how to get to us, and told them to return in half an hour, during which time we all lay quietly on our beds. When the three returned we sent them out the window to the roof, with directions to stay at the top, holding the ridge-pole, as the slant was steep. At the end of the ell was a gnarled old sumac tree, the branches of which almost reached the lower edge of the roof, and Katrine and I demonstrated how not to slide down too fast by clinging to the shingles with toenails and fingernails, and we were soon in the sumac tree and on the ground very near the water. We went down the shore to some mammoth oak trees that hid us from the house, and on the pebbly shore we rushed into the water, exulting in the moon-light and in the blaze of phosphorescence that sparkled on our white skins at every stroke. We decided to stay all night, but after a few long swims we were shivering with cold and returned to our tree. M. was heavier and less athletic than the rest of us and could not get onto that lower branch, and no amount of pushing and pulling on our part was of any avail. " You go on in," I said to the three on the roof, and Katrine you go and unlock the kitchen door and I'll get M. around there." The maids had gone to bed, and we sneaked past their doors, passed the nursery where Jennie and Louise and Jack and Elizabeth were sleeping, and were at last in the secret passage, frozen but exultant.

Next morning we thought up the wonderful idea of going over to camp on the island. The Melloons had left for the mainland and the house had been empty for some years, and had never been locked up or entered. After some conversation our parents gave permission with certain conditions. The island contained about forty-five acres, and we were not to go boating on the far side, or out of sight up the creek without permission; also we must realize that Papa and Cyrus were very busy repairing leaking walls and Mama was taken up with the garden and two younger children; that there was a great deal of labor involved in living in that deserted house on the island, and that we wouldn't have much help. Undeterred we rowed across with brooms and dust pans. As we forced the door open, we felt that we needed spades as well, for a great deal of plaster had fallen down in chunks, and the Melloons had left old cardboard boxes, rags, trash, and broken wood. Where to put it all? The room we entered had the rusty cookstove, and beyond this was a little area that was more of a vestibule than a room, but it was separated by a door, and we decided to sweep everything into this area and shut it off. On one side of the kitchen-living room was another room into which we decided to put the cot mattresses, and as that contained less debris we started there. Saving what might do for kindling, with our hands and our brooms we soon filled up what we now called the buttery, and jammed the door shut — not to be opened again. Two rooms were now moderately clean and we had opened one window — the rest were jammed and some had broken glass, into the openings of which we stuffed some of the rags we had found on the floor. We returned to the mainland for lunch and our little brother Jack consented to help us, which meant that we could load two boats at a time instead of one. There were five of us, and in the attic there were only four cot mattresses that we could take, but

Katrine and I could manage with one, and Jennie produced the oldest blankets she could find. Two of us stayed on the shore of the island to carry up mattresses that came one at a time in the boat, while Jack delivered coal and buckets half full of water in the second boat. We had promised not to pull up any of the well water for any purposes (Jack had discovered eels in it), and so what we carried across was only for drinking, and we had already practised washing dishes on the shore with pebbly sand, salt water and rockweed, and it worked. For washing ourselves the method was to be the same, minus the sand. We had a boiler and a fry pan, some eggs, bread, potatoes and canned food and some candles and we felt quite ready to move in, but there was a difficulty. Katrine had promised to play the violin at a concert in the Careys' new music room, and we felt it would be mean to move without her, and so would wait till after the concert and move over in the dark.

My mother and father drove Katrine home in the carriage and it had started to blow and to rain a little, and we were urged to wait for daylight in the morning, but we had our rubber coats on and I said we would go now as there were only five days left, and we started out. I felt that this going out into the river in wind and rain and darkness was very terrific, more exciting than anything in the adventure books; but I had a vague feeling that all the others did not feel as I did. We beached the boat and could just hear Papa calling through the megaphone, " Are you all right? " " Fine," we screamed back, and tied the painters to a rock and walked up to our new abode. There were no electric torches in those days and we worked in the dark to open the front door, now jammed by the dampness; finally managing to pull it free after prying with a hammer that lay on the step. We had candles perching on every shelf and on the stove, but matches had been forgotten, and helped by the flashes of lightning we lay down on our mattresses, fully dressed, with sweaters on, and we pulled up our blankets, one each. We were tired and wanted to sleep, but terrific thunder and flashes of lightning added to a whistling of the wind through the cracks in the broken windows kept us awake. Soon the thunder lessened and I dozed, only to be waked by a very weird sound. From the top of the roof, not over our heads but at the back, came a sort of scraping and bumping, then a thump. The others were awake too, and were whispering. "It's a wild animal," said one. "It's a big eagle," said another, "I hear its claws and its wings." But the thump that followed was too heavy for that. "It's a man, and he's breaking in on us," said Beth. "Nonsense," I said. "People don't break into houses like this one, and no one is going to get here in a boat in a wild storm like this; someone has to go out and find out what it is." "You are much the oldest, and you thought this up," came from under someone's blanket, and there seemed to be a murmur of approval from the other blankets. My damp bathing suit was hanging on the door knob and I put it on and went out the front door. I was truly afraid, but as I walked toward the back of the house the brilliance of the lightning and the crashes of the thunder made it more exciting than frightening. There was, we had decided, no tree near the house, but when I came to the back I saw a big old half-dead apple tree that we had forgotten or been too busy to notice. One huge branch had been recently broken and was dragging over the roof; when a gust came, it was lifted, to land with a thump. This was too good to be true, and I ran in to tell the others. "We are lucky," I said, "to have a good roof — most campers are right out in the rain." "They have a tent," said someone. "But a tent blows down in this kind of wind, and they sleep on the ground. We have mattresses." "Go to sleep," said someone.

But I was being seized by one of my moods of exhilaration. Here we were on a deserted island, completely responsible for our own survival, no one was back of us; we were on our own. (I had forgotten that in the morning our little brother would bring coal, water, and milk.) We were superior to terrible storms. We had left civilization behind us. We were monarchs of all we surveyed. We were a part of this lightning and of the sky and the sea. And so, feeling at one with the universe, I turned over on my half of the hard mattress and dozed off.

The lightning finally petered out and we slept soundly to wake up early, feeling very hungry. We had found our matches and I filled the stove with bits of cardboard and wood and started a lively fire for our fried eggs. There was a crash — the back of the stove had fallen off, and most of the fire was on the floor. This struck us as so humorous that we were weak with laughter and could hardly clear up the blazing bits. Fortunately a tin sheet was still in place to protect the floor, and we swept up the coals into the frying pan and bread pan to lay them outside on a wet rock.

Sue was opening five eggs and was shaking them up in a milk bottle, and with eggnogs, slices of bread and butter and a banana each we made a good breakfast on the stone step at the front door. As the Melloons had had no closet, there were endless hooks on all the walls and I had noticed a very long piece of black wire looped on one of them, perhaps an old clothes line. After putting this through two holes in the back that had fallen off the stove, this piece was suspended from projections on top, the bottom was bound around and around under the oven, and our stove was perfect.

At this moment Papa, who had been wondering what the severe storm had done to us, appeared at the door. He couldn't help laughing at the stove, but thought it would do, and with a mysterious tool that was in his knife he tightened my wires so that there was no longer an open crack in the back of the stove.

Then we told him about the awful scare on the roof, and we all went to look at the offending tree. Papa had an axe in the boat and in no time that big heavy branch was chopped off and sawed up into lovely bits for the stove. He opened a few jammed windows and asked if there was any box out back that we might use for a table. As we didn't want anyone to look " out back " we said " No " very definitely and later on Cyrus came with a low box from the boathouse, which just held our five tin plates. Then, having gained permission, and having told where we would go, we rowed to the wharf to get the tiny catboat which just held five of us, and we sailed forth for a picnic lunch, armed with canned meat, bread, apples, and milk.

Can there be a more lovely thing than a rocky cove with a little white sailboat anchored on its blue waters? This cove at the back of the island was formed by two points of pinkish rock, and above this the ledges rose high, topped with white pines and cedar trees. Every bit of it was paradise which we drank in to the full while we dove from one point to swim to the opposite one and repeat the process. We had left the food in the boat with our clothes, and it was with some difficulty that we swam with it to the nearest shore. It was damp but unharmed, and we made beef sandwiches, drank lukewarm milk and ate apples. This was the Life. There was no doubt about it — it was the " Best ". After about two hours of this we decided that we were getting too burned, and we swam back to the boat. I could get to the deck over the rudder and helped to haul the other four aboard, pulled up the anchor and sailed around our island to the family float, where our row boat awaited us.

As we thought about supper, I said, " We've got to cook those chops before they go bad." " They smell awful now," said Sue. " We won't eat them," said Sophy. " Nonsense," I said. " We can't waste all those good chops. They've only been here one night." The girls all went outside and soon reappeared. " Did you know," said one, " that bad meat shines in the dark? " " I know it doesn't," I said. " You come down in the cellar and see," said Katrine. The cellar was an indentation in a rock foundation at the back of the house. Three steps led down to its four-foot area, and one had to stoop to enter. In one corner was a pro-jection of rock on which we kept our meat and milk. It was dark down there, and the muddy floor was still wet. " You look," said Sue, and she held out the cake pan in which reposed our chops. I couldn't believe my eyes, but, sure enough, the two chops on top were sending forth a slight glow. " Let's get out of here," I said crossly. " You bury them or throw them overboard."

I think a year had gone by before I learned of the trick that had been played on me. Those girls had rubbed the two top chops with the ends of matches and the phosphorus had shone in the dark.

That night the apple wood burned well and we ate canned ham with eggs and toast and hoped for potatoes, but they never cooked through, and we took them all back to the cook next morning. This worked to our advantage, as she felt that we must be starving and always referred to us as " Those poor dears ", and every day there was a casserole dish for Jack to bring with the buckets of water. He was too little to carry them up, but left them on the shore, and one day we forgot to go after them and the tide rose as it always does. The drinking water was spoiled, but the baked egg had had a glass cover and a little salt water only improved its flavor.

That night when I went over to get drinking water and milk I passed a few cigarettes in an open dish. I put five in my pocket. That evening after supper I announced that I had a treat for all. As we had no lamps to read by and no chairs to sit on we were in the habit of going to bed very early, but this time I lighted a candle and produced the cigarettes. We sat on our mattresses, our backs against the wall and we puffed with glee. Our previous experience had been with soap bubble pipes filled with sweet fern, and this had not been successful. Twice I blew smoke from my nose, and then I felt sick. " I'm keeping half for tomorrow," I said; but from that day to this I have never tried another cigarette.

The five days flew by with a new adventure for each. Sometimes we climbed the huge rock near the house to picnic on top. There were new ledges and groves to be discovered all over the island — sometimes we took the big row boat and, with two pairs of oars, went far up into Sagamore Creek. Our camping trip had been a complete success, but we were rather tired. When the day came for our return, we meekly submitted to hot baths, shampoos, and clean dresses, and we openly enjoyed the lamps to read by, the comfortable chairs, and the sheets on the beds. But as I dropped off to sleep I knew that that other world would always be there. That world of beautiful unknown thrills — of oceans and islands and rocks and canoes and sailboats and maybe some day even mountains.

Many years later I returned to the island with my husband and three children for summer vacations. Papa had installed a pipe under the river that brought water to the house and we had added two sleeping porches, a kitchen and a bedroom out back. It was amazing how closely the adventures of my child-hood were repeated by my children, even in the same boats, for many happy years. Now when I see my grandchildren camping in Maine, I know that the heritage is still there and that the spirit of the Portsmouth Island still carries on and always will.

Chapter VIII

CRAZY WOMAN

A T THE END of Little Harbor Road, near our gate posts, lived the descendants of the man who had sold the Mansion to Papa. They were kindly and fond of us all and we were fond of them. I was at their house one day being treated to cookies when Grandma Cushing asked whether I had heard about the crazy woman who had escaped from the asylum. I had not, and didn't feel much interest until our neighbors James Roosevelt and Pat Sturgis came in, in great excitement.

" What do you think, there's an escaped crazy woman, and they think she is on the Little Harbor Road, and there is a reward of $10 for anyone who can report where she is. We thought we might see the road from your kitchen, and if she came by we could report her without having to go near her."

Grandma Cushing was a good sport with a sense of humor. She loved a prank, and, as she winked at me, a diabolical, vague idea flashed into my head — some sort of mental transference was reaching me from her mischievous wink. She said to the boys, " No, you can't see the road from the kitchen, but if you go to the edge of my woods you can see a good distance and you might go on the road a little way and see her coming. Anyway, eleven-year-old boys can run faster than any old lady — you eat some of those cookies and I'll be right back with a plan for you."

As she went out into the hall I could see by the motion of her head that I was to follow, and on the stairs she said, " Do you remember that time you came into my parlor and acted so crazy you scared us all? Well, this time you can dress the part."

She had a costume closet which she seldom had an opportunity to enjoy, so she was thrilled as she opened the door to take down what consisted mainly of her own worn-out black silk and satin clothes. She quickly gave me a long skirt that covered my bare legs, and bed slippers for my feet. An old satin cape looked too dressy, but she turned it wrong side out, showing shabby cotton patches, and on my head she put a flat, torn black hat, with a huge chiffon veil hanging over my face. This had taken no time, and she told me to run out through the kitchen door and go around the corner out of sight on the road.

When alone on the road, I began to feel very nervous — more like running back than like waiting for the boys. The newspaper had said that the escaped woman had been seen on Little Harbor Road. This was bordered by woods and rocks, and it seemed as though her face were peering at me from the back of each boulder, and next a bony hand and a leering eye would seem to appear from behind the trunk of a big pine tree. I wanted to be anywhere but where I was.

And now there was the rattle of wheels; a carriage was coming and the occupants would surely take me in and return me to the Insane Asylum. But the sound of wheels died away into the Carey driveway, and I breathed again.

In the meantime Grandma Cushing was advising the boys to take a chance on that ten dollars. " If you get around the curve you can see a good way on the road," and out they went.

I was still feeling uncertain about the sound of wheels and the thought of that asylum, and when the boys appeared in the distance they looked so big I felt sure they were men come to pick me up, and again I was tempted to run. When I saw that it was James and Pat, I was so relieved I longed to hug them—I did not want to make them share the dreadful feelings I had been through. I did not want to frighten anybody. But this was Grandma Cushing's game; I must play it right, and I fell into the part.

I swayed a little, gesticulating with my fingers and wailing loudly that I was a poor old thing who was lost with nowhere to go, with no friends but cats and squirrels, and that all I owned was a water faucet that went round and round and round while the water never ran.

The boys were so startled and amazed that they did not move, but stared at me for what seemed many minutes. They seemed in a trance, and then they ran, not back to the Cushings, but in the opposite direction, across the fields to their own homes.

I returned to take off my black clothes, and Grandma Cushing was disappointed that the boys hadn't come to have a good laugh over our having fooled them.

I told my family about having dressed up like a crazy woman, but they hadn't paid much attention until Mr. Sturgis drove in with some eggs, and asked what we should do about the escaped woman. " Pat is in an awful state," he said. Then Mrs. Roosevelt, who lived very near us, came in wondering whether the police had been notified. " James won't sleep tonight. He is in a panic." They were talking so fast they couldn't hear my parents saying, " Don't worry, it was only Molly," and wouldn't believe it when they did hear.

It ended in my having to drive back with Mr. Sturgis to explain everything to Pat, and then he drove us to the Roosevelts. Both boys said the same thing — " It couldn't have been you, with those long bony fingers she was waving about." But they finally believed me and slept well; though I had a feeling that impersonating a crazy woman was not all that it was cracked up to be — not so humorous after all.

Later we made it up to Grandma Cushing by dressing up in all her costumes and making up a play for her.

Chapter IX

SCHOOL

DURING our early years at Winsor School there were of course no cars, and when there was snow the streets were a paradise. Cabs on runners were called booby huts and had a lovely place to hold onto on the back, and the grocery pungs had an outside edge on which one could sit. When these sleighs passed at a good clip we used to go punging, grabbing the side or back, to stand on the runners, often for many miles.

Once I was having a pung ride on the back of an open sleigh with a pair of horses and two men on the box, when I saw that the back seat was full of fur robes. I crept in under them, and was enjoying life as the horses pranced down Commonwealth Avenue, when the footman looked around and spoke to the coachman. He stopped the horses and pretended to lash out at me with his whip, saying, " I don't know what Mrs. Gardner will do to you." " My father is John Templeman Coolidge," I said; " a great friend of Mrs. Gardner's. She would invite me to stay."

But I doubted this last, and while the footman was shaking the snow out of the furs, I caught a butcher's pung that was speeding homeward.

But during school recess we were not allowed to pung or to have snow fights, and I was feeling very repressed one day when a schoolmate's hat was blown off by the wind. She was an older girl who was very dressy, and her hat was covered with large birds' wings, which I resented. I picked it up and threw the whole thing towards a passing booby hut. To my complete amazement the hat flew into the open window and the cab turned the corner of Berkeley Street and disappeared. The girl, in tears, went straight to Miss Winsor, and I was, as I expected, sent to the office.

" What possessed you? " said Miss Winsor. " I have no idea," I said; " just a sudden feeling; but it's an awful looking hat." " You've got to learn to control such feelings, that hat is gone, and it cost ten dollars. What can you do about that? " This was a new and terrible aspect of the situation. I only had $3 and was saving up for a new camera lens. " Sometimes," I said, " I earn money bringing in coal from the back alley." " Our coal is all in the furnace room," said Miss Winsor. " You can now go to your class." My classroom was on the ground floor, and as I reached the landing there was something going on at the front door. A lovely lady was holding out a feathery hat to one of the teachers. It seemed that on hiring the cab to go down town she had picked up the hat from the floor, and showed it to the driver. All he could think of was that he had passed a group of children near Arlington Street. " We'll pass the Winsor School on our way, and I'll have a try there," said this intelligent lady. What a reprieve! I had to stay indoors for three days of recess, but that was nothing. I could finish my homework.

When springtime came we had the run of the Public Garden in recess time, playing hopscotch, prisoners' base, etc. One day I was climbing up on the base of a statue to get a long jump down, when I found that, if hoisted by two friends, I could reach the stirrup of the gentleman on the horse and could get my fingers through with such a good grip that I felt sure of going higher. What a joyful prospect this was of sitting behind the General on that prancing steed. But the stirrup seemed to be the last good purchase, and I was sliding back, down the slippery bronze trouser leg, when a policeman came along and told me in a very rough and rude manner to get right down out of there. He even pulled me down, talking crossly all the while. I happily found that I had a piece of chalk in my pocket, and when he turned I made a large white cross on the back of his heavy overcoat. He walked away and we were all laughing hilariously when he met another policeman who turned him around and brushed his back with his gloves. Then they turned to look at us, and I very stupidly took off my worsted tam-o'shanter and waved it at him. He went straight to Miss Winsor.

The result was awful. The entire school was summoned to the assembly room for a speech from Miss Winsor in which she announced that someone had disgraced the school, that we had been allowed to use the Public Garden as our playground, and that now, through the outragious behavior of one girl, this privilege was likely to be taken from us; and she added that the lack of a playground might involve the necessity of moving the school away, which might mean ruin, and she ended by saying she did not know who had brought this upon her. Katrine says that I raised my hand and said, " Please, Miss Winsor, it was me." My punishment seemed headed to expulsion when my father, who was on the Art Commission, went to City Hall and reported to Miss Winsor that that policeman had no authority to keep us out of the Garden, and that higher authority had no plan of doing so. The incident had not even been reported. I was on probation, but could not remember this for very long, for when a new grammer teacher came to school I took a dislike to her and took all the advantage I could. One of her mottos was " Laughter and Learning don't go together."

Shortly after her arrival she saw me laughing in the back row and asked me to go to the board and write a sentence with a noun, a predicate, an adjective, an adverb, and a pronoun.

She was over six feet tall and very plain, and I wrote, " The tall and handsome Miss Johnson has arrived in town." There was a burst of laughter which angered her, and I was sent to Miss Winsor, with expulsion again on the horizon, but Miss Johnson was inadequate and left, while by some miracle I stayed on.

Miss Elizabeth Winsor was a wonderful teacher and beloved by all. She was very beautiful and really cared about getting

Latin across to us. No one wanted to misbehave in her classes. But my favorite teacher was Miss Leslie Hopkinson. She was so sympathetic and so easily amused that we did not want to go against her or tease her. One day, I can't remember what I had done, she had cause to tell me to stay in my seat during recess. I knew she was being fair, but I was tired of studying and grew very restive. It was raining and the girls were playing a game in the downstairs hall and I strained to hear what the laughter was about. Holding the seat of the chair tight against me, I walked to the top stair and found that by leaning far over I could walk down — chair and all. Half way down I met Miss Hopkinson coming up. She gave me one look, burst into peals of laughter and continued to the top without a word. I sat in my chair and umpired the games, walking up again in the same position when recess was ending.

When it comes to Miss Paine, I wish she were living that I might apologize for the misery I must have caused her. She was the math. teacher and a very good one, but very strict indeed. There was something about the clamping down of authority that used to make me feel so restive that something had to break through. A balloon man went by at the close of recess one day, and I bought four gas balloons, giving one each to three cooperative friends, with certain directions.

When we were in the midst of proving that X=Z I raised my desk top; theirs opened also, and our four balloons floated beautifully upward. " Take them right down," said Miss Paine, but the strings had been cut and they wafted about till they reached the very high ceiling, where they stayed for several days, till they withered and fell, two during a class.

One day Miss Paine gave us a problem about A going down the river at a certain rate when he met up with B going the other way, so how fast was the tide running? I couldn't think, and my eye wandered to the closet door, which was ajar. On the corner of a shelf was Miss Paine's little black bonnet, edged with black fluff. I slipped in and put it on, tying the little strings under my chin, and there was the cape on the hanger — I put that on, too, and gesticulated as nearly in Miss Paine's way as possible. Soon all eyes were on the closet; those who could not see beyond the door were moving over. Miss Paine heard suppressed sounds, and turning from the board she walked straight into the closet, her face red with emotion. This was not caused by my mis-behavior, but by the fear that her precious things were being harmed. She took them from me very quietly, laying them reverently in their places, and as I look back I believe she had made them herself, and that the black satin cape, lined with bed quilting, and edged with black fluff, with loops instead of buttonholes, was probably her only winter coat. She did not send me to Miss Winsor, but I was to stay after school to do some more problems about A and B on that river. This meant that she had to stay also, and miss the horsecar that carried her home.

I was beginning to take it in that Miss Paine was really a human being, that she might not like her job but had to earn her living, and I was ripe for improvment when Mama told me that Miss Winsor had been to see her again to say that I was still a very bad influence in the school, that I was demoralizing others, and had been kept only because my work was satisfactory. Mama pointed out to me the fact that I had wonderful friends where I was, and a change would be very hard in every way. I don't think I had ever faced the fact that I might really have to leave, and now I knew that this was the last thing I wanted — and I did better from then on.

Two years later I happened to do something that pleased Miss Winsor. The French department at Harvard was planning to stage Racine's *Athalie* on the grand scale, magnificent costumes from Paris, splendid actors. Miss Cushing, who was to take the part of Athalie, was almost a professional, and Prof. Sumichrast, the head of the department, was experienced in acting. Four other professors and sixty students from Harvard and Radcliffe made up a large cast. They had not yet found a child to take the part of the young King Joas, and were having tryouts in various private schools.

Papa was on the visiting committee of the French department and Prof. Barrett Wendell, who had seen one of our plays, sent my name to Prof. Sumichrast and I was invited to his house to tea. I had some hangover of a French accent, though one of the newspapers later called it " quaint ". The professor had me read a few pages while he went down the hall, said my voice carried, and would I take the part of Joas.

I said I would ask my mother, and she said I must consult Miss Winsor. I was greatly surprised by the pleasure that Miss Winsor showed over my having been chosen for the part. She said she had assumed that Miss May's school would win out, because it specialized in French and Miss May was to play the long part of Joas' mother. She said that going to Cambridge and back for rehearsals would take a great real of time and that I could be excused from all French classes and preparations.

My part was not a long one and I used to sit on a front seat of the bleak, empty theatre, doing my home work till I was called to the wings to be ready for an entrance.

My big time came during the four performances that packed the theatre. During the grand finale I had nothing to remember, no more to say, while, surrounded by the whole cast, including thirty Harvard boys and as many Radcliffe girls, I was raised to my high throne and proclaimed King. The wicked queen was being held by the guards, the Cecilia Society and some of the Symphony Orchestra were playing inspiring music, and each night I forgot that this was fiction. I took upon myself all the credit and all the glory of being the true King. My exaltation was at a peak and it was hard, after such heights, to return to being an ordinary everyday school girl.

Chapter X

THE GIFT TREE

As Jack was seven years younger and Elizabeth fourteen years younger, they could not have a very frequent share in our adventures, but we used to have a game — especially when our friends were visiting, of kidnapping Jack from his crib while Jenny, our wonderful nurse, was still sleeping. We used to take him to our bedroom to play games, in which he bounced about from one bed to another; then Jenny would appear to say he was not warm enough and take him back to the nursery. He was always awake long before Jenny was and, on lovely mornings, we would take him out in a boat, or give him a ride in his cart, when Jenny always maintained that the wrapper or sweater we had grabbed up in our haste was not sufficient. Jack now says that we gave him a wonderful time, though sometimes a bit on the strenuous side. Once I whirled his cart on too sharp a circle, and he fell out and broke his collar bone, but though we also took him and Elizabeth out in the carriage with the pair, this is the only accident I can remember.

When Elizabeth became old enough to kidnap, Jenny had become a veritable protecting dragon from whom we could seldom steal her charge. She and Jack were charming, beautiful little children and Katrine and I used to enjoy getting up little entertainments for them. One of these was the annual " Gift Tree ". During the winter we would save little odds and ends that might appeal to Louise, Jack and Elizabeth and put them in a box to take to Portsmouth. There would be bits off the Christmas tree, also little things we could well part with, marbles and gumdrops, and we would decide to spend a quarter on each child. There was no " Five & Ten " store in Portsmouth in those days, but, when July came around, we decided it was time for "Gift Day" and we drove to town to a newspaper store that often had marked-down toys. They produced some wonderful jack-in-the-boxes that were dusty and had nicks on the paper of the boxes, but were otherwise in good shape, springs and all. They were marked $1.00 each — and I said we only had seventy-five cents for three of them. "Well — that paper on boxes don't look too good, you can have them" — and we walked out triumphant. On arriving home we washed the boxes and pasted new colored paper on the torn places and rejoiced in our bargains. There was a little dog for Louise, who loved dogs, and when the box popped open he rattled, suggesting a bark. Jack's was the usual little clown, and Elizabeth's a cat, the squeak of which suggested a meow.

Mama asked us not to tell the children till next morning that it was to be "Gift Day" — as last time they had lain awake in their excitement and then been out of bed much too early.

Next morning was bright and fair and hot, and we went, as soon as the sun had risen, across the fields to the woods where the chosen Gift Tree rose behind a flat rock. Standing on this rock made it easy to reach even the upper branches. First we hung all the gumdrops, through which we had sewn threads. They had become rather sticky, but, as Katrine said, this made them more shiny. Then came the marbles, on each of which we had pasted a bit of adhesive to hold the strings. The sun made them shine in a very satisfactory way. Then from our paper bags came the little objects we had been saving, and they added up to more than we remembered. Once Katrine said, "I don't think I'll part with this after all." I said, "Then if we start on that we'll end up with too little. If you keep that little horse, I'll keep my little boat," and we left everything on the tree, and decided it was the most beautiful we had ever had. The jack-in-the-boxes were lined up on the rock in front of the tree — each in a different-colored wrapping of gay tissue paper.

Feeling that it was all very perfect, we returned to the house and told the children that this was " Gift Day ", and their joy was a delight.

Jack said, " Do you mean *this* day today? " We said we'd go and see in about one-half hour. " What makes you think there'll be a tree up there? "

" We can go and see."

There had always been an element of mystery about Gift Day. No one knew how or why it came — no grown-up had ever been to the celebration. It was secret.

We soon started off across the big field, Elizabeth in the little buckboard, Jack helping to drag it; Louise with Barney, our big St. Bernard, Katrine and I behind to see if they could find the little gap we had made in the stone wall. Finally Louise and Jack had found it, and we left the cart, and walked into the woods and up the rocks. Jack shouted, " I think I can see the tree." " There's something shiny way over," said Louise, and they ran up the round rock to the flat rock, and I put Elizabeth down so that she could run close to the tree and squat beside it. She had first choice, then Jack — then Louise, then all over again and soon the paper bags we had given them were nearly filled with marbles, gumdrops and small toys. " We ought to have a present for Barney," said Katrine. Louise said she had a cracker for him and also gave him some gumdrops and caramels which made his teeth stick together and set us off in roars of laughter.

Now it was time for the big surprise and we pointed to the square boxes at the foot of the tree. "The blue one is Elizabeth's," and she took it. " The yellow is Jack's, the green is Louise's and Barney's." She had hers unwrapped first and Barney whined when the little dog barked, setting off another burst of merriment — Elizabeth kissed her little cat and Jack loved his clown, and everyone played for some time before I asked a favor.

As it was not easy to get everyone up to the woods I had brought my camera, in hopes of getting a few photographs of fairies and wood sprites. We had a way of making garments, or wreaths that sufficed as such, out of oak leaves strung together with their own stems. Katrine and I made a few of these and I suggested that as we had lots of time before going home I would like to get a few pictures. Katrine very obligingly put on a belt and wreath of oak leaves, in place of her clothes — and Jack did the same, though rather grumpily. Louise was sitting against a rock with Barney at her feet. She was sucking two gumdrops, the white strings of which were hanging down over her chin, and she flatly refused to take anything off. " Fairies or no fairies." She said that last time she had posed for me I had got her so scratched up by making her sit in the juniper that she still had the marks. I let Elizabeth play with her cat, because my lens had no shutter, and she seldom stayed still long enough for me to take the cap off and on.

I took one of Katrine down in the juniper bushes, looking up at Jack, who was standing — also one of Katrine alone, and one of Jack alone seated on a rock. When I developed them I thought they were so beautiful that I would have some enlarged for Christmas presents.

When we had returned to Boston that autumn I took my negatives to a Kodak shop to have enlargements made, and the man said they would make beauties. I was to return to pick them up with the glass negatives, but time went by and one day my mother went shopping.

As she walked down Bromfield street, she passed the large window of a Kodak shop and something caught her eye. Sure enough, there in the front, close to the glass, was a 10 x 12 enlargement of Katrine in oak leaves, next an equally large one of Jack sitting on a rock, looking very grumpy, his only cloth garment being a large bandage on his cut finger. Next, another large one of Katrine and Jack together. She was squatting in the juniper so as to look more his size, smiling up at him, and he down at her, both scantily clothed in oak leaves.

Mama walked in and asked about them, and the man said the little girl was going to return to get her negatives and enlargements. " In meantime I made those big ones for my window, and lots of people are interested in them; lovely aren't they? "

Mama agreed that they were, and said she would pay the bill and take the big ones as well as her daughter's order and negatives. When she gave them to me, I was quite disappointed. " Now," I said, " I have no Christmas present for you and Papa, and anyway they have on plenty of leaves for any window." Mama said that it was better not to be in the public eye in shop windows whatever one had on, and that it was a great compliment to my photos to have the professional admire them so much. I felt better about it and the photos went into a book, and I made a new Christmas present.

Chapter XI

GRAMPA AND INDIAN PLAY

GRANDFATHER PARKMAN, my mother's father, used to spend part of July and all of August with us in the Wentworth Mansion. He used to write History in his bedroom a good part of the day, but each day when the tide was right he would row off to go fishing in the decked boat that my father had had built for him by our friend Bert Treffethan. Grampa was very lame, and sometimes walked with crutches — sometimes was wheeled in his chair down the gangplank and helped into his boat. I often went with him, and he liked to do the rowing; but if his shoulder hurt I loved to slip into the bow seat, up behind him, to row him out and anchor off a rocky point where the perch and flounders were most likely to bite. He used to give me his knife and I would cut up the clams on the edge of the boat. One day the blade slipped and, to my horror, I could see the white bone handle plummeting down toward the dark bottom. Grampa said it didn't matter, and I cut the bait with clam shells. He said this brought us better luck than ever, and he pulled up a fish with its eye caught on the hook. As it approached the boat the fish flapped off, leaving his eye on the hook. Grampa lowered this without adding any clam and quickly pulled in again. The big perch had no right eye, his own eye had been the bait that caught him, and from then on I ceased to be sorry for any fish. They were " hard boiled ". This had been a real thrill, and as we rowed home we forgot about the knife.

I had a shabby one of my own and that afternoon I sand-papered it and oiled it and held it to the grindstone; and that evening, hoping against hope that he would not want it, I handed the result of my labors to Grandpapa. He said " Thank you," and put the oily thing into his pocket. Next morning Cyrus went to the city to buy oats, and at lunch time, after Grampa had been helped into his chair and his crutches were propped up in the corner, he called me to his side, put his arm around me, and handed me a cardboard box. It contained two beautiful knives with white bone handles. " One for me, one for you," he said. I had never hoped for such a lovely thing.

The following winter Francis Parkman died, leaving a raft of grandchildren and a world of enthusiastic readers. I had been reading the " Oregon Trail " and was writing a play to be acted in a field the following autumn before school started. We all felt confident of our abilities, as we had been producing a play every winter in West Medford for Mr. Hallowell's birthday. There were four Bennetts, two Hallowells, and two Coolidges to portray an Indian family and a trapper's family who were having a terrible feud, in spite of the fact that an Indian lad and a white lad were fast friends. There was to be a great deal of arguing, a great deal of fighting, and capturing of the trapper's family, and a great deal of galloping on bareback horses.

During the summer we were to produce costumes, each with an allotted share. Esther Hallowell and I would be the Indian chiefs. I had a leather jacket with leather fringe that Esther was to have copied in tan cotton flannel; Ruth and Manie were to be squaws and they made quantities of bead necklaces and floppy robes and ribbon and bead headgear. What really interested Ruth was the making of four Indian rope bridles with nooses to fit over the horses' lower jaws. My work was to produce Indian headgear for the two chiefs that would be truly striking, and this did not, in anticipation, seem too difficult, as I had been collecting hen feathers and turkey feathers from the butcher and had gay cotton headbands to sew the feathers to, and into the inner edge of these headbands was to be sewn some black horsehair to hang down around our faces. It seemed that it would be easy to get horsehair as some horse must have had its tail cut recently. We started off on our search, asking at livery stables, at the butcher's, the milkman's, at the express; but no one had a horse's tail. Finally we went to the blacksmith and he said he had just the thing. " Pat's hoss died yesterday and it had such a thick tail of hair he pulled it out; we got no use for it ", and he produced something that made us scream. It was a thick black tail, but from it there protruded a long bloody root. " Don't blame you," he said and he took an axe to most of the root, leaving a good bit to hold the hairs together. This he held under the pump and, rolling it in a dirty newspaper, handed it to me. We drove home in triumph and I took my treasure into the living room, to find on unwrapping it that there was considerable root left. " Oh," said my mother, " we'll rush to the pump." After another rinsing, Jennie volunteered to take the object and wash the whole thing with soap and hot water and hang it in the sun. It was a beautiful thick tail and I added an inner band to the feather headdress and sewed in the hairs as I cut them off. Half of the remaining hair I mailed to Esther, and the photographs show that our headdresses looked striking and truly authentic.

Three weeks before the family was to move, we went to the Bennetts in Wayland to rehearse for the coming play. We knew our lines, and the hardest thing to be learned was the leaping to the horses' backs and galloping off. There were, of course, no saddles, but each horse had a tight surcingle to which we could cling while jumping as high as possible, to land on our stomachs on the horse's back. The thing was to make this stomach landing a thing of seconds before the right leg swung over. It should appear that we had landed from the ground in one motion as the horse galloped off, just as the Indians did in Buffalo Bill. We thought we did pretty well, and during the final performance we at least never had to repeat the leap.

At last the great day for the dress rehearsal had arrived, and with darkened faces and plumes flying we started off, some in the carriage, and four on horses to the lovely flat field that was to be our stage. Thick pine woods made the background and an Indian tepee was our only scenery. On our way we had to cross a railroad track and the gates were down — the train almost stopped as passengers rushed to the platforms. " They never slow down that much," agreed the Bennetts. " They think we are real Indians," and with a feeling of elation that we were just about real, we approached our field and started to turn in where we had taken down the bars, but my horse wouldn't turn and veered to the right on a different road. As we had only had three horses that were not too high, the local minister, Mr. Heizer, had very kindly lent us his polo pony, which fell to my lot. I had ridden it with the bridle that came on it, and my bridle now consisted of a braided rope with a slipnoose that went over the horse's lower jaw. He had guided well by the neck, but now there was no question of guiding or of slowing down as the pony took things into his own hands. Head forward and down, he tore off on the dead run taking sharp turns on roads that were unknown to me. My only ambition was to stay on, and the surcingle helped some. Suddenly we turned in at a wooden gate and were approaching a stable. We rushed up the ramp and the pony planted his four feet, to slide all the way across the stable floor. He had taken me home to his stable. Mr. Heizer was directing a carpenter and they both jumped to one side. " That is a terribly dangerous thing to do," said Mr. Heizer crossly, but as I was in full regalia, he soon realized what had happened, especially when he took a look at the bridle. " This horse has a very hard mouth," he said. " You can never handle him with those strings." " But Indians do," I said, almost crying, " and he guides beautifully by the neck." Mr. Heizer began to realize that I had been run away with, and was very shaken, and that I had to get back to the dress rehearsal. " I don't know the way back, not one bit of it," I wailed. " You have a good drink of this milk while I get my saddle on; I'm going back with you, and that beast of yours will stay with my horse." He handed me a tin of warm milk just in from the cow, and I felt better. I never felt more grateful to anyone and he produced a bridle with a curb bit and a chain that went under the pony's lower jaw. "Don't you ever take this horse out again without this bit, Indian or no Indian," he said. "I'm keeping this rope affair." We rode back to a very successful dress rehearsal with a small audience to applaud our every move.

The day for the final show was bright and fair and the train had had directions to stop at the gates on the road to let out the audience from Boston, while others drove from Weston, Lincoln and Concord; more than we could have hoped for. All went well and when it was all over Aunt Lizzie Parkman, Grampa's devoted sister, told me how pleased he would be to know that we had used his trappers and his Indians in our play, and that it made her feel happy too.

Chapter XII

CRUISING ON *THEO*

OUR NEIGHBOR Mr. A. Carey was a man of changing moods. He had been painting in Paris with Papa, and on his return to America he fell in love with Little Harbor and bought a large piece of our land and built a house on Sagamore Creek. He soon decided that he would never paint well, and would become a musician; so he bought a fine cello and had a large music room added to his house. He soon decided that his ear was not true enough to play in tune, and hung his cello on the wall. Inspired by Papa's love of the sea, he had the perfect knockabout built by Lawley for cruising. She was a lovely little 21-foot sloop, high sided, with two bunks, and room for two on the floor on each side of a central folding table. She was named " Theo " after Theo Middlemore, a beautiful lady whose husband owned the Orkney Islands, where Papa and Mr. Carey used to visit when abroad. Papa and Mr. Carey went cruising together, and as long as Mr. Carey had Papa with him, cruising was the most divine experience in the world.

But Papa was too busy to go constantly, and Mr. Carey hired a boatman whose company he did not especially enjoy. This man could handle the sails and so could Mr. Carey, but neither of them were sure of their position on the chart. Pleasure boats had no engines in those days, so when one was becalmed in a fog it was hard to know where the tide had taken you.

The *Theo* soon ran on the rocks outside of Little Harbor, but fortunately the Coast Guard, who had seen her go out, heard her horn and with ropes and anchors pulled her off on the rising tide. After several mishaps, Mr. Carey let his boatman go and sailed only when nautical friends were visiting him or when Papa could go along. After two or three years of this, he decided that he was no sailorman and tried to give the *Theo* to Papa. He could not accept it, but a satisfactory sale was arranged, and *Theo* was towed around, to be pulled up and propped up on our beach where we all scraped and sandpapered and painted till she was ready to go in again. There followed cruises and adventures that were among the many highlights of our happy lives. My first trip was to go with Papa to Kennebunkport to visit the Delands. We had a brisk, lovely sail as far as York, where the wind left us completely and we slammed about off York and Cape Neddick for what seemed hours and I was very seasick. As I think of subsequent cruises, this always happened at this spot, but I always knew that we would soon be in the more sheltered waters of Casco Bay. This time, as dark was approaching, we rounded the rocky point to turn into the narrow entrance of Kennebunk River. The Delands were on their float with open arms, and after a good supper we anchored *Theo* in the river and went to sleep on the blue denim of the mattresses. This was a lovely way to live, and next morning I cooked scrambled eggs on the small vapor stove. We carried our water in big jugs, and so did not use it on dishes, but with a chain and saltwater soap, even hard egg will clean off in the ocean.

We sailed home with the assurance that *Theo* was a wonderful boat and could take us anywhere.

Two friends were coming to visit soon and Papa agreed to a cruise in Casco Bay. With permission from the parents we were off, fortunate in a strong breeze that took us all the way to Falmouth Foreside, just beyond Portland, where the Misses Longfellow welcomed us and gave us milk and fruit for our early morning start.

In the morning Papa suggested that, as we had had such a very long sail the previous day, we might go to Jewell Island for the night. We upped anchor and after sailing for about an hour we approached the high rocky point of the island. We were sheltered by its woods, had no wind at all, and a strong tide was rushing from the rocks into which Papa was heading. I was up on the bow and called out, " We can't go in there, it's too narrow." But Papa called to me to take the tender and tow us in. In the meantime he had the sail down and the girls were each pulling an oar. As Papa steered us through it seemed that we would touch the boulders on either side, but we soon rounded them and saw that we were in a miniature river, wide enough to swing in; but as we looked ahead the far end of the river ended in a pebbly shore. We were in a minute cove surrounded by cliffs on one side, pine woods and rocks on the other. We cast our anchor and the shelter was complete. No winds or waves could reach us here. It was a remote world of our own — a fairyland of wonders, and we spent the day swimming and picnicking and exploring the woods and coves of this lovely island while Papa made some repairs and enjoyed having his boat to himself.

Next day we sailed in a good breeze across the sparkling waters of the Bay to anchor in the Basin that was like a beautiful landlocked lake.

After washing up next morning, Papa suggested that we row out to find a creek that Professor Sargent was interested in because of the arbor vitae trees that grew wild there. We took a picnic lunch, found some of the trees, and broke off bits of branches to wrap in a wet towel for the Professor, and Papa marked the spot on the chart.

We had been gone a long time and the tide was dead low before we returned to *Theo* and, on entering the Basin, were appalled to see that she was lying on her side high and dry. " I gave her too much rope," said Papa; " now we must wait till the tide starts to lift her and see that it does not go over the low side and swamp her. He and I stepped out onto a muddy kelp-covered area and walked to *Theo* to get the spare anchor and the halyard, of which he tied the ropes together. The two girls in the tender rowed us out as far as the anchor line and halyard allowed, and we dropped the anchor to give us a steady hold to haul from. With every rising inch of tide we pulled on that mast till the *Theo* began to float and we could board her again. There was a terrible mess in the cabin, but no damage except that our cans of food had been lying in bilge water and every label was soaked off. From then on we ate what we opened first. If it turned out to be fruit on the first try we saved it for dessert, but a second fruit had to be eaten on the main course.

On following days we went to Cundy's Harbor and up the Sheepscot River, all different, all magic, beautiful places.

We bought provisions in tiny harborside shops, and after five glorious days we decided that, with no engine, we were far enough from home, and we sailed back to Little Harbor, full of our adventures.

Soon after all this Papa asked me to do something that made me feel pleased with myself. We had sailed to York to spend the night there, and on entering the rocky inner harbor at low tide he told me to take note of that difficult entrance, and to check with the chart. I think he felt that fog might be coming in, for next morning it was thick as pea soup, and we could hardly see the bow of the boat. He had a friend arriving in Portsmouth and we left *Theo* with two anchors down and took the train home.

Next day was clear, but Papa found that he had to go to Boston with the friend about buying a painting for the Art Museum. This could not wait, and to my surprise he asked me if I would like to go to York without him to bring *Theo* home. I would, and he said I must have someone along. The only friend available had never sailed a boat, but would be able to steer when I had to go forward.

We took the train again and found our tender at a fisherman's landing. The man was there and said that Mr. Coolidge had asked him to give the boat to no one. It took some explanation to persuade him, but we did at last, and finally had the mainsail up and were tugging at the anchor when another difficulty arose. One of the anchors would not budge, and it was only with the help of the fisherman that it was pulled in, bringing with it a huge rock wrapped with mud-laden kelp. This had brought us too near to one of those projecting rocky points, but we had the sail up, made a right-angle turn and out of the tiny inner harbor, and to my relief were soon in the open sea with a rousing breeze. That made us feel like uplifted beings. As we heeled way over in the dashing spray, we were in tune with our lovely boat and with the sea, the sun and the sky.

We stayed well out from the reefs of that dangerous shore, turning only when ready to aim for the centre of Little Harbor, where we would find our buoy and our mooring. But there was no buoy, the extra high half-moon tide had sucked it under, but after circling many times we found it, covered with rock-weed, and brought it up with the boat hook. *Theo* was safe at home, and we had had a most glorious sail.

Papa had many cruises on *Theo*, when he could enjoy his own friends as well as his daughters. A gentleman told me that he had gone to Marblehead for Race Week and was looking down the hill at the harbor, when his companion said, " There are four boys on that little knockabout anchored near shore, and they are having the most wonderful time. Let's go down and see them." The four boys were my father, Mr. Henry Vaughn, 6 ft. 4, Henry Wadsworth Longfellow, 5 ft. 4, and Clipston Sturges, all living on *Theo* for Race Week.

I know that Papa's enthusiasm for boats and for all that they bring carries on in our sons. For five years they had a cruising boat that took them into most of the harbors in Maine, far into the St. John's River, and into many Canadian harbors. They often took us along to rejoice in such places as Pleasant Bay and to that beautiful Rogue Island. We bathed on its steep sand beach and climbed the high rocky headlands that bordered it and gave it the prize for the loveliest of all the islands.

After our boys sold the *Mary C* they cruised on friends' yachts, often on Dr. Alex Forbes', going as far as the Bras d'Or Lakes, and once across the ocean to Naples. Also they go on friends' boats on ocean races, around Geoffreys Ledge, to Bermuda, to Halifax, or to Mackinac Island. Papa's love of the beauties of the sea and of the game of mastering it to serve man's ends is a heritage that is alive and is always marching on.

Chapter XIII

JAPANESE PLAY AT DUBLIN

WE WERE by now in 'midteens, but, as we had determined not to grow up, this adventure can still be classified under " childhood ".

Uncle Joe Smith had a grand idea of putting on a very fine play, which was to raise money with which to buy ice for American soldiers training in Cuba during the Spanish War. A letter came to Portsmouth that caused great excitement, as it stated that Katrine and I were to be the hero and heroine, and would we, in a week's time, come to Dublin for a ten-day visit of rehearsals and preparations. What joy! All our immediate enterprises were dropped and, with our freshly ironed cotton dresses (no evening things required) and our bathing suits all in small bags, we travelled to Dublin.

The Smiths lived on a point on the lake and, off the avenue, before reaching the house, Joe had built a recessed Roman theatre, the seats circling above a sunken stage, and we had assumed that the new play would be here.

" Too small," said Joe. " We will have a huge audience this time," and he led us down to the lake. On one side of the point was a Japanese garden with hillocks, rocks and pools, dwarf evergreens and stone pagodas from Japan. It was on the edge of the lake, on one side of these gardens, that the audience would be seated, and we were startled and thrilled to hear that our stage was to be the lake after dark.

The boundaries were to be an island on the right, and, on the left, there was a small pier or jetty behind which we could be hidden before making our appearances.

Mr. Smith, Joe's father, was as clever at carpentry as his wife was at producing costumes. Next morning, as we sat on the pebbly beach to hear the plans, we were startled to hear Joe say, " Daddy, by tomorrow I'd like an island on the lake about there," and he threw a stone. " Not too far for you to lead a wide or double plank to shore, a little under water for Katrine to walk on. There's to be a pagoda on this corner of the island big enough for Katrine to stand in, but no rush about that."

We sat entranced, to hear that Katrine was to be a Japanese princess who had been captured by a very wicked magician, Mr. Russell Sullivan, who kept her imprisoned in the pagoda on the island. By some magic intercession she could walk on the water to bewail her fate near shore.

I was her prince who tried to accomplish her escape, but was always thwarted by the magician or by his servant, a huge dragon — Uncle Joe, of course.

Though we could not rehearse till the island was in place, there were plenty of properties to be made. Mrs. Smith handed me the cover to her ash can, which had a good handle, also a can of gold paint and a pile of chains, usually for use in cleaning kitchen pans. " Gild all this," she said, and she gave Katrine a pair of flat shoes with square knobs of wood which were to be glued and wired to the soles, to raise her to water level above the plank. When the gold paint had dried, Joe painted a big black dragon-rampant, and I had a beautiful shield. An old mop became a spear with an end of flaring straw.

Wherever Joe travelled he brought back lengths of gay cotton, or pieces of beautiful brocades, not new enough for clothing, but perfect for costumes, and we decided on a lovely white silk kimono with pink and blue flowers for Katrine, and a bright red and gold brocade that would become a jerkin for me. The gilded saucepan chains became part of a helmet and some chain mail to go around my waist and legs, coming down under the brocade.

As to the dragon's head, Joe made the most stupendous golden thing — four feet long with jaws that would open and shut, huge eyes and flaring nostrils, and a jagged crest standing high above its forehead.

Next morning we ran to the lake before breakfast, and we quickly suspected that Mr. Smith may have had an old raft hidden somewhere, for there, just where Joe had thrown the stone, was a half-finished island with rocks and loam and strips of moss piled about.

" Joe, how much greenery do you want out here? " asked his father.

" A little more loam, and I'll bring the dwarf trees."

After breakfast we wandered in the woods and collected small pines and cedars, which Joe bent and wired to imitate the curving Japanese ones; and with more loam and rocks the raft had become a Japanese garden.

" The pagoda on this corner has got to look like stone." So we put sand in the gray paint, and it did.

Then the two-foot plank was led to the mainland and Katrine found she could walk on it. As Joe had been a little dubious, this was a triumph.

Next day we three rehearsed in our bathing suits, and the college boy who was to be my boatman came to paddle my boat from the stern, while I stood in the bow with my spear and shield. It was hard to balance, and Joe thought it might be effective to have the dragon push me overboard during the first part of the battle. We tried this, but when my boatman had hauled me back we decided it made a rather awkward and un-dramatic scene, and that I was to stay victorious in the boat. " But now," said Joe, " you know just how to go ahead if you do lose your balance."

The great night came, and, as was always the case with Uncle Joe's plays, the weather was perfect, and there was a moon. There was no electric light in those days, but Mr. Smith had lime flares and searchlights rigged in place.

Joe and I, with my boat and boatman, were hidden behind the

jetty, and Katrine was in the pagoda, the magician behind it, when the audience started pouring in. As we peeked between the piles it looked like multitudes, and soon Mrs. Smith gave the signal and Mr. Smith turned a spotlight on the pagoda. Katrine came out and walked on the water, the reflection of her white kimono shimmering under her. We could hear gasps from the audience while we held our breaths, fearing she might slip on her raised clogs, or step over the edge of the submerged plank. She made two trips to shore and back, to wild applause. Then the magician appeared from behind the pagoda and, to her supplications, answered that she was a prisoner for life, could walk on the water but could never go ashore.

When he had gone, I appeared, standing in the bow of my boat. I was hoping that my red and gold brocade was making as good a reflection in the limelight as Katrine's white one had.

I tried to reach my princess, but the magic power of the magician prevented, and, swearing that I would soon return to find the dragon and kill him, I said farewell.

As my boat turned, the searchlight was disclosing the horrible golden head of the dragon. Shouts of applause, and the fight was on.

As the huge head lunged at me and a claw grabbed at the boat, I nearly lost my balance, and twice I dropped my shield to the bottom of the boat, to clutch the side and continue jabbing with my spear until I could straighten up again. This seemed to me a terrible mistake, but turned out to be very effective as seen by the audience.

After a hard fight, the spotlight went out, and in the darkness, smoke and brilliant red fire belched forth from the dragon's eyes, nostrils and jaws. Joe had started a red light, balanced on a shelf in the dragon's lower jaw. I thrust at this till it was at last extinguished, the head flopped over and Joe kicked himself free and swam to the jetty, where the second boatman helped him to shore. He was very tired.

My boatman took me to the princess and I lifted her aboard, and we were paddled straight out, to disappear in the moonlight.

In the meantime the magician, who had been standing on the end of the jetty in his glorious blue and red brocades, with the spotlight now on him, was proclaiming that, as all was lost, the only thing left for him was Hara-kiri. He opened up his big kimono to disclose a huge round pink stomach, which he gashed open with his dagger. Pink and red rags fell out, and he very courageously fell straight backward into the lake. Laughter and loud applause. His packed stomach gave him so much floatage that he could not turn over to swim, and the second boatman towed him to shore.

The audience assured us that it had been the loveliest and most exciting thing they had ever seen, and we felt that all was well.

Next morning Joe's throat was very sore, and Mrs. Gardner, who had been spending the night, as she never missed a Smith play, insisted on getting a doctor. He said that Joe's throat was not burned by the red fire, as we had feared it might be, but had been irritated by the smoke, and it soon healed. Joe told me that twice I had nearly drowned him, for, just as he came up for a gasp of air, my spear had pushed him under, but that it was worth it, as the battle had surpassed all our hopes.

He was jubilant over the financial success of the play, as, in addition to the ticket money, there had been many extra donations. " Think of the thousands and thousands of cakes of ice that will buy," he laughed. I don't think I ever had a clear idea as to whether that ice was to go to Florida, Cuba, or Spain.

Many years later my husband and I went to Dublin for Joe and Corinna's fiftieth wedding anniversary. Their granddaughter had gilded her own Ford car for them to be transported in, to a reception at the Catlins', and, rearing from the top of the hood, was the original dragon's golden head.

Chapter XIV

COUNTESS OBENDORFF AND OTHERS

O NE DAY Mr. Carey told me that his sister, Madame de Steurs, was coming to visit, bringing her daughter who was near my age, and would I come to lunch on Friday. I went with my usual bare feet and cotton dress, a clean one, and my hair was brushed, but, as I approached the group on the porch, I felt rather inadequate. I was introduced to Madame de Steurs, who was very tall and stately with stiff skirts that rustled when she moved, and she had on many large jewels. Margot was also tall, with long rustly skirts and hair pinned to the back of her neck. She started the conversation by saying she was only a year older than I. " How awful," I thought; " but I will not be like that in a year." Mama had suggested that I invite her to go sailing, and not being able to think of anything else to say, I came right out with it. " I have a sailboat of my own. Do you want to go for a sail with me this afternoon? " " Have you a boatman? " asked Madame. " Gosh, no," I said. " Molly is a skillful sailor," said Mr. Carey. " I have been out with her, and Margot would be quite safe." " She can't swim," said Margot's governess. Then Margot spoke for herself and said that she hated the water and didn't like the way boats tipped. So that was that. At lunch I was between her and the governess, and they both asked me about certain books and poems, none of which I had heard of. Then I produced my last effort. " We have two saddle horses; do you want to go riding with me? " " And your groom," said Madame. I could not help laughing as I imagined Cyrus in that role. " We have an old man with a red beard; he cleans the horses and boats, but he can't ride," I said. " You have a side-saddle," said Margot. " Oh, no — they are not good for the horse; the weight on his back is not even. We have a Mexican saddle and an English; you can take your pick."

By now Mr. Carey may have thought the conversation was not going too well, for he suggested that I take Margot to see the Wentworth Mansion. This I did after lunch, and she was tremendously interested in the council chamber and billiard rooms, in the stacks of guns against Indian raids, in the cellars where they hid the horses, and especially in the slaves' rooms.

As the Mansion had been open to the public before Papa bought it, sightseers still came occasionally, and our friends loved to make up stories for them. There was a queer hole under one of the slave's built-in bunks and Molly Lowell fabricated a wonderful story about its leading down under the river as a tunnel of escape. We had almost forgotten that this was a figment of Molly's imagination, and I told Margot about it. When we returned to the living room my parents greeted her, and she exclaimed over the beauties of the house and place and said she was going to write a story about that tunnel under the river through which the slaves used to escape. Papa started to speak, when Mama gave him a look, and they both gave me a piercing one. But they said nothing, and I was very grateful to them. Mama asked Margot to lunch with us on Sunday and she said she would accept with pleasure in her rather stilted English. Katrine appeared, asked Margot to come to see the barn, and we walked up the hill.

When our friends came to visit, we used to take great pleasure in turning our goat loose on them as they dodged through one door after another, terrified by the branching horns that looked so dangerous. Once he had them pinned to a wall, Billy would lose interest.

When Margot stopped to fix a shoe lace I whispered to Katrine, " We'll keep Billy tied up." " We will," she said.

Katrine led the colt out. Margot was delighted. She knew a

good deal about horses and said she had jumped a low hurdle. Katrine put the bridle on Ruth, jumped onto her back and cantered off.

Margot seemed amazed that she had not waited for a riding outfit, but had gone in a cotton dress with bare feet and not even a saddle blanket. After showing her Diamond and Gypsy and Billy, we walked back with her and she said she must now rest and study, and she thanked us for a delightful occasion. " Aren't you sorry for her," said Katrine as we walked home. " That long stiff dress." " She may like it that way," I said.

———

Thirty years later my husband was to work in New York for a good part of a year, and we rented our house and I took our youngest son, our daughter and two of her friends to Europe. After travelling about we settled in Lausanne, where Mac and the girls were to go to school as boarders. During a few of the winter months Mac's school moved to Gstaad for the skiing and climbing, and I moved up to a pension where the girls could come to enjoy those beautiful mountains during week ends or vacations.

Returning after snow had gone, the pension in Lausanne seemed rather drab, and a change that offered itself seemed a tempting one.

I was invited to a reception at the house of Dr. and Mrs. Vitoz and, on being introduced to various ladies and gentlemen, found them all immersed in one subject, " The Countess is coming." " Madame D. has been to her villa." " It is very beautiful." " She is an art connoisseur and has wonderful tapestries and paintings." " And the grounds and the views of the lake and the mountains." " Epatant." " And here she is." A tall, stately woman in a handsome fur, large jewels and a rustling skirt was making a grand entrance and was being introduced to the eager guests. When it came to my turn I thought she looked familiar, but I must be careful — " Have you been to America? " I said. She started a little, said, " I am half American. Why do you ask me that? "

" Did you know Mr. Arthur Carey? " She turned white and grabbed my arm. " Uncle Arthur, dear Uncle Arthur. Those happy days! Who are you? "

" I am Molly Coolidge and you are Margot de Steurs."

" O, you are the little barefoot girl that Uncle Arthur was so fond of." I laughed and stood aside for others who were waiting to be introduced.

But she was soon back and asked me to come to lunch next day. She asked for my address, as she would send her car to fetch me, and she had something very serious to ask me, and then she left.

Next day a large, old-fashioned black car with furs on the seat, and a chauffeur in fancy livery, was at the door of my pension. The man, looking dubious, asked me if I was the lady going to the château of Countess Obendorff. I was driven through a park and up to a lovely white building, the central part of which had two stories of pilasters with wings of one story on either side. I could see that the wooded grounds reached down to the lake, with the mountains looking very high behind it.

Margot was very welcoming and introduced me to a nice little girl with Alice-in-Wonderland hair, and to her English governess, Miss Jones.

The tapestries and the Louis 16th furniture were lovely, and so were the paintings, but with too many cupids and roses for my taste.

We sat by the fire while I admired the surroundings and congratulated her on her daughter. " She is named for me, but we call her 'Margette' — and I have a big son who is tutoring and seldom here. The Count has arranged a very good match for him, the girl, his fiancée, is lovely — you will see her, as she lives here in Lausanne.

" You will see her, because I want you to come and live with me here."

This was very sudden. I didn't know what to say.

" This is awfully nice of you, but I would have to check about the girls' vacation plans and about my room at the Pension."

" I am very lonely; I want so much that you should come. Take my car and go to Brillanmont and to Rolle, and tell me that you will return."

The girls were most enthusiastic about such an adventure, and felt I mustn't miss an opportunity to stay in such a beautiful place. " Where is the Count? " " That's what I don't know," I said. Mac felt as they did, on condition that this plan did not interfere with our week-end expeditions, and I promised that. I would not have missed them for anything.

After arranging to give up my room for a while, I called the Countess on the telephone and accepted her invitation, and packed a bag to move next day.

At supper at the château that night I was amused, as I had been at lunch, by the menu card, which was large and in a very elaborate silver frame, and was passed from hand to hand. A small amount of meat had an elaborate French title, while details such as prunes, rolls and nuts had separate lines to themselves.

After supper Miss Jones and Margette went upstairs, and Margot got out her petit point and started right in with her story. She said she had seen that I noticed the strange menu card, and that that was an example of how she had to save and scrimp. She said the Count had taken a huge dot and, ever since their marriage, had been giving her papers to sign which she could not understand, and that by now she had signed away most of her property, and that he gave her an allowance which was scant on which to run this big place.

" Where is he now? " She didn't know, maybe in Berlin; but

he might turn up at any time in a white car driven by a chauffeur who had been an officer in the Indian army and wore a white turban and robe, and was huge.

"When they come, I know they will try to kidnap Margette," she sobbed. Then she told me about the plan, and wanted to show me the arrangements right off, and instruct me on what to do when I saw the Count's car. We went through the cellar into an alley that led on to a back drive, on which there was an old barn. "Michelle lives there and has the second car in which he will drive Margette and Miss Jones away." She showed me the bell that would be heard by Michelle, and I promised to help them escape as well as I could.

That night I dreamed that the Count came, and that at the corner where the tunnel and the back drive met he was overtaking us. I tackled him by his knees and he fell long enough to enable Michelle to drive the girls away in safety. But in real life I never saw Count Wilhelm Franz Marc von Obendorff.

The girls used to come, and Mac and some American friends, but I never felt that I contributed very much to Margot's pleasure till M. Bori came to see me. He was a charming Swiss gentleman who knew that he was going blind and, while he could still see, had climbed every high mountain in Switzerland. As soon as I introduced him to Margot the sparks seemed to fly. He lived in Coppet on the estate of Mdme. de Staël and, as he had been a trustee there, he had the entree to the château at any time at all. Soon they were quoting Mdme.'s poetry to each other, and there were plans of walking in the Coppet grounds next day, and of going in to see Mdme. de Staël.

"What do you mean by that?" I said.

"Oh — don't you know?" It appeared that her husband had been so entranced by her beauty that, when she died, he had had her preserved in some liquid, and she could still be seen through a glass cover, by the especially privileged. Margot had never been, and was delighted by the prospect; but when they invited me to

[74]

go with them, I was glad that I had a good reason to avoid it. I was taking the young people across the lake, and up the funicular to the " Rochers de Naye."

Some weeks later, when Bori came, Margot was shopping with Margette. " I have some good news," and he told me all about it.

The Countess had told him that in a certain bank in New York, in the hands of trustees, she had part of her Astor inheritance of which the Count knew nothing. She did not dare to try to have any of it sent to her, because he would be sure to hear of it. She had willed it to Margette and the son, but she wanted the income for her life. Bori had suggested that he could have the income sent to him. Already a letter had gone from Margot and a favorable cable had come from the New York bank which had heard from Bori's bank. Every month after that Bori brought a packet, and Margot sported a mink coat, and the meats were no longer stews.

Bori also told me that he had met the Count recently at a man's dinner and did not think that he was the villain he had been painted. A big, rather jolly man, very selfish, but probably with no intention of kidnapping the child. When she becomes of age he is to plan a suitable match, a titled one.

Margot had cheered up considerably and I stayed on for another ten days, following my own plans while she followed hers.

She was interested in hearing that I knew Lady Hood, whom she had met at the English Embassy, and I told her about Gstaad.

On our first morning there, Mac and I had been out on the wooden porch of our Pension rooms seeing the breathtaking view, when the owner came up to say that Lady Hood was outside and would like to speak to me. She said she was too snowy to come in and that we must come out to go lugging. She was dragging two sleds, and her son, Mac's age, had two more, one for each of us. We were soon walking part way up the mountain to coast down again, then trying the side roads, which were all steep, and we were thrilled by being in such a glorious place. She said she would come next day before there was any more snow, to climb part way up the mountain behind our Pension. As she was delayed, it was nearly three before we started with Mac, Zander Hood and J. Saltonstall, all ten years old. We walked for an hour, stopping to look through vistas in the woods at the beautiful mountains that rose all about us, when Lady Hood said we must now return as we must not be on the mountain after dusk. She called the boys, who were just ahead of us, and they returned without Mac. " Where is Mac? " " He went on ahead." " Oh, no," said Lady Hood. " Run up to that next ridge and call as loudly as you can, then come right back, Zander; how could you let him go alone? " " I didn't," said Zander. " He just disappeared."

Just then a man with a pack on his back was coming down the trail and I asked him if he had seen a little boy. " Yes, with American boots on; he said he was going to the summit." " What is it like up there? " " Very steep, a narrow peak of rock with a sheer drop." " Tell them at the Pension," said Lady Hood, and we walked down fast. As the trail grew clear she told the boys to run ahead alone and tell them at the Pension. I didn't see the point of this till we met three men coming up with ropes. " There's another search party on the back trail," said one man as they hurried on. There was a horrid air of tension in the Pension as we entered. It was nearly dark and a group of schoolboys was also being equipped to search.

Lady Hood said she would wait a bit. After a while, one search party returned, having seen no one. Then another, when, most casually, walking in at the front door came Mac and a very attractive man with whom Mac had been to the summit. They had come down on a third trail. " I met him near the top," said the man. " I was going up to get specimens, and he promised to stick close — there are bad places up there."

Lady Hood thanked him and she said to Mac, " I want you to come to see me tomorrow; there is something very important that you need to hear about." I went to the door to say good night and she said, " Thank God " and dropped a tear. Mac's nice scientist ran out the door and walked down the steep hill in the dark to Lady Hood's hotel.

Mac heard plenty about the dangers of being separated from one's party when on a mountain and he never did it again, but he wrote to his father a long account of the scenery, and of the nice scientist who had explained everything to him. " I had a wonderful time but I'm sorry I was such a worry to Lady Hood and to the search parties and to Mother, but I couldn't be so near the top of a mountain and then go home and say I had never climbed a mountain in Switzerland."

Lady Hood was wonderful to us. She was in the Grand Palace Hotel, which had a beautiful outdoor skating rink not open to outsiders but she arranged for us to have the use of it, including the three girls who came every week-end from Lausanne.

I had taken a few lessons in waltzing, and one sunny morning I was practising outer edge forward, change, and outer edge back. An attractive man was sitting on a bench, and when I needed a rest and sat on a bench on the opposite side, he came and sat beside me. " Lady Hood told me who you were, Mrs. Perkins. I am Captain Mackenzie and I've been watching you skate." " Not much of a treat, I'm afraid; can you waltz? " I said hopefully. " Not even an outer edge, but to tell you the truth I am not as interested in your skating as I am in your skirt. How does it happen that you are wearing the Mackenzie plaid? "

" Well," I answered, " I walked into a large department store and picked out the prettiest plaid on the counter. Our family's is the Forbes plaid, but it's dark and better for the city — this is my gay country skirt." Captain Mackenzie slapped his leg and roared with laughter. " I think you Americans are the funniest people I ever heard of; you have your clan plaid, and you walk into a department store and buy the Mackenzie plaid," and he continued to laugh. Then he asked me how I happened to know Lady Hood so well.

" I don't," I said. " She used, before her first marriage, to live at times with my husband's family. It is out of loyalty to and affection for them that she is doing all this for us. She had never set eyes on me till she came to the Pension with the sleds."

That week-end the girls came up from Lausanne with Gypsy outfits, as there was to be a costume ball at the Grand Hotel and Lady Hood had invited us all to dinner, with her two daughters and their husbands and another son.

In the middle of dinner Lady Hood said, " Here comes Mackenzie straight for you, Molly." I looked around and there was the Captain, handsomer than ever in his Scotch uniform, and with him were two beautiful little light-haired boys, dressed in black velvet jackets with all the fixings of full regalia — lace shirts, sporans, dirks, socks to the knee — and their kilts were of the Mackenzie plaid.

" Mrs. Perkins — this is Stuart and this is Donald, and you can see now how I feel about the Mackenzie clan."

" I do indeed," I said, and I will never forget how you look now — you three. Tomorrow I will dye my skating skirt."

"Oh, no," said the Captain. "That is a beautiful piece of tweed. It would be an insult to the Mackenzie plaid to dye it. You won't, *please*." " She won't," said Lady Hood — and her children said, " She won't," and mine echoed, " She won't."

The Captain slapped his leg and laughed again and said they would now go to bed, but that he would return for the dancing; which he did and introduced my girls to all the young men.

———

I told Margot about this, and she liked to hear about our many excursions: sometimes standing in pungs with our skis, sometimes being dragged by four horses with strings of sleds out behind. As her childhood and youth had included nothing of this kind, she was rather wistful about it and said she had no courage. " You could have had if I could have trained you when you were six years old."

" Well, I'm glad you couldn't try," she laughed, " I'm only fit to look at the scenery from the back of an automobile. I don't like danger."

Three years later Bori wrote to me that the Countess Obendorff had been killed in an auto accident, and that Margette and Miss Jones had been taken to Berlin by the Count, where they seemed to be happy.

Soon Bori came to America to live with our American friends in Milton till his death. He gave French lessons and had plenty of companions to give him a guiding arm on his daily walks. When he recounted his narrow escapes on mountains he used to say in his broken English, " at this point my ice pickle slipped," much to the amusement of all. He was a dear man.

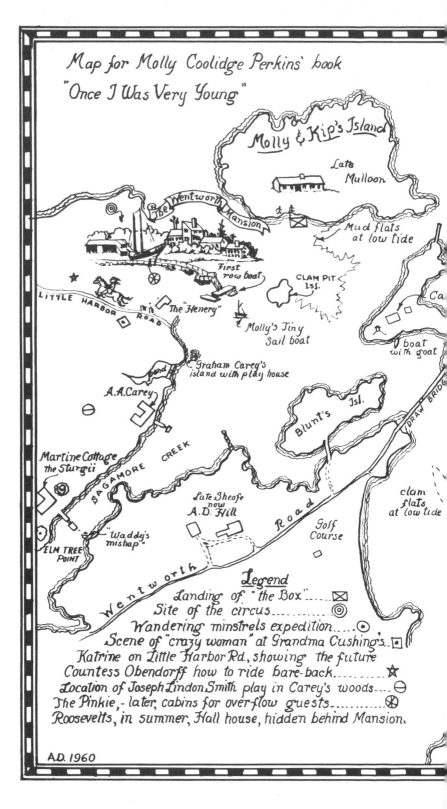

Map for Molly Coolidge Perkins' book
"Once I Was Very Young"

Molly & Kip's Island

Late Mulloon

The Wentworth Mansion

Mud flats at low tide

First row boat

CLAM PIT 1SS.

Ca

LITTLE HARBOR ROAD

The "Henery"

Molly's Tiny Sail boat

boat with goat

Graham Carey's island with play house

A.A.Carey

pond

Blunt's Isl.

DRAW BRIDGE

Martine Cottage the Sturgii

SAGAMORE CREEK

clam flats at low tide

ELM TREE POINT

"Waddy's mishap"

Late Sheafe now A.D. Hill

Wentworth Road

Golf Course

Legend
Landing of "the Box"................⊠
Site of the circus.....................◎
Wandering minstrels expedition.....⊙
Scene of "crazy woman" at Grandma Cushing's.▣
Katrine on Little Harbor Rd., showing the future
Countess Obendorff how to ride bare-back..........☆
Location of Joseph Lindon Smith play in Carey's woods....⊖
The Pinkie,- later, cabins for over-flow guests............⊗
Roosevelts, in summer, Hall house, hidden behind Mansion.

A.D. 1960